Priest and Bishop

Biblical Reflections

PRIEST AND BISHOP

Biblical Reflections

by

Raymond E. Brown, S.S.

Wipf and Stock Publishers
EUGENE, OREGON

Wipf and Stock Publishers
199 West 8th Avenue, Suite 3
Eugene, Oregon 97401

Priest and Bishop
By Brown, Raymond E.
Copyright©1970 Society of St. Sulpice
ISBN: 1-57910-277-8
Publication Date: January, 1999
Previously published by The Missionary Society of St. Paul, 1970.

Reproduced by permission of the Society of St. Sulpice, 1999.

CONTENTS

TO

PATRICK W. SKEHAN

PROFESSOR OF SEMITIC LANGUAGES

THE CATHOLIC UNIVERSITY OF AMERICA

In gratitude for what I have learned from him
both about the Bible and about priestliness.

PREFACE

This booklet has a very limited goal. Its size should forewarn the realistic reader that no complete, scientific treatment of the biblical background of priesthood is envisaged. Perhaps the word "reflections" in the title will convey my approach and intention: I have culled the Scriptures to offer material for thought at a crucial moment in the history of the Roman Catholic priesthood. With the whole Christian world looking on, we Catholics have entered a sometimes acrimonious debate with ourselves as to what should be expected of those who are in the special ministry of the Church, i.e., the priesthood—What manner of life should our priests live and what work should they do? Also under review is the role of the bishop, said traditionally to possess the fullness of the priesthood. We are asking whether the authority structure on all levels should be more collegial or democratic and what such a change would mean in light of the traditional theology of the episcopate. Ecumenically we are pondering our relationships to other churches in which there is no episcopate in apostolic succession.

In all these debated questions proponents of very different positions are resorting to Scripture for justification. For some the whole goal of the priesthood is summed up in the words of Jesus at the Last Supper, "Do this in commemoration of me"; and in their minds bishops have the same authority as the apostles to whom they are the successors. Others, when they think of apostles, think of Paul and his clarion call to freedom; and when they talk of priests, do so in pseudo-Bonhoefferian terms as "a man for others," often understood without sufficient qualification. In my judgment, the appeals to Scripture emanating from both extremes tend to be shallow in their grasp of the biblical origins and ideals underlying our priesthood and episcopate, and so I have attempted here to supply biblical information that should go into the modern discussion. Of course, biblical information cannot solve the questions being discussed. (A description of origins can be a definitive solution only to a fundamentalist who does not believe in Christian development beyond the 1st century.) Nevertheless, the biblical information must play an important part in our decisions and we must remain loyal to our NT origins. This does not mean that we are so subject to the NT picture that we cannot effect change, but that change is to be introduced only knowingly and with extreme care. Without that type of loyalty to the NT we risk becoming a Church that is no longer apostolic.

Were this a major work on the priesthood I would have to write first on the Church and fit the special ministry or priesthood into the larger complex of the ministry of the whole Christian community. But in this brief sketch I deliberately leave many aspects of the priesthood unexplored and touch only the main lines of development, with the expectation that perceptive readers can extend the implications of my remarks to the areas not discussed. In short, I hope that my reflections will serve both as a guide and an incentive to reflection on the priesthood by others, both clergy and laity.

The immediate origins of the two chapters that make up the booklet may be of interest. The chapter on the biblical background of the priesthood was called forth by a request from the personnel board of a large diocese. The board was discussing with younger priests their possible assignments as associates to certain pastors but was encountering on both sides difficulties reflective of very different understandings of what a priest should be and the tasks he should be asked to perform. Sensibly the board proposed a discussion of the priesthood, with one paper, among others, treating of its biblical origins. Subsequently I was able to use in other dioceses the ideas I presented on that occasion, and I found that they seemed to help priests in clarifying their own positions. The second chapter about the bishops as successors of the apostles consists of reflections catalyzed by two different types of experiences. At times, in speaking to

groups of diocesan priests, I have been dismayed by the lack of
understanding that seemed to separate some bishops from their
priests. Naturally there are many factors involved in such situations; but, especially where good men were involved on both
sides, I wondered if the problem was not related to the concep-
tion of the episcopal office. The unqualified idea that the bishops
are the successors of the apostles and therefore responsible for
all the major decisions of the Church forces the bishops to
decide authoritatively in such a variety of fields that, simply by
the law of averages, many of their decisions have to be lacking
in information and wisdom. It occurred to me that perhaps a
careful delineation of the differences in NT times between
bishops and apostles would reduce to a more plausible level the
expectations of what a bishop should be, with the consequence
that bishops might cease both to attempt the impossible and to
be criticized for not achieving it. The other area of experience
that contributed to Chapter Two was ecumenical contact. I have
served in the international dialogue on apostolicity conducted
between the Vatican Secretariat for Promoting Christian Unity
and the Faith and Order Commission of the World Council of
Churches, and I have also been engaged in the national Luth-
eran-Catholic dialogue on the eucharistic ministry. In each the
claim that bishops were the successors of the apostles was ex-
amined closely for its implications about the validity of ministry
in non-Catholic churches. Thus I came to see that both for the
internal health of the Roman Catholic Church and for its relationship to other Christian bodies it was imperative that Catholics know some of the limitations of the claim that the
episcopate stands in apostolic succession.

I have no illusions that what I write in these pages will
satisfy all. Some will be disappointed that the treatment is not
more detailed and scientific. However, my preference for a
booklet over a book has been determined not only by the limits
of the time I wanted to devote to this subject but also by my
conviction that the readers I wished to reach would be more
open to succinct reflections than to anything formal or exhaus-
tive. A more crucial dissatisfaction with some of the ideas expressed in this booklet will be felt on both ends of the Catholic

theological spectrum. Conservative readers will be dismayed to discover that the traditional ideas of the origin of the priesthood and of the episcopate are questioned in the light of historical evidence. It is somewhat shocking to see how simplified a picture was painted in Catholic circles without real proof. On the other hand, liberals may be angered to find me pointing out that many of the traditional ideals of the Catholic priesthood have a firm biblical basis and that much of what they would like to write off as Victorian or medieval happens to stem from the demands of Jesus of Nazareth. Let that be as it may. If Scripture is the word of God, it is a two-edged sword—and in modern times that means it cuts both conservative and liberal. If I have done nothing more than to make the two extremes a little less certain that their views are true to Scripture, then I have done my duty. Wherever I have moved from biblical exegesis to applications reflecting my own experience as a priest, I wish the personal character of my convictions to be taken into account, so that they are not pretentiously cloaked with "scholarly" authority.

As for the non-Catholic reader who may pick up this monograph to find out what a Catholic exegete thinks about ministry, it may be wise for me to state clearly that here I am not concerned with (and hence not disparaging) other forms of ministry that might have emerged from the varied NT situation; rather I am interested primarily in what did emerge in the Church of which I am a member. I make no apologetic defense of the papacy, the episcopacy, or the priesthood, but accept them as given institutions of grace within the Roman Catholic Church whose development has been guided by the Spirit. (I am not so naive to think that every development within the Church is the work of the Spirit; but I would not know what guidance of the Church by the Spirit could mean if it did not include the fundamental shaping of the special ministry which is so intimately concerned with Christian communal and sacramental life.) My problem is, granted the existence of these institutions, what light do the Scriptures cast on what should be expected of them both by Catholics and by non-Catholics.

CHAPTER 1

THE BIBLICAL BACKGROUND
OF THE CATHOLIC PRIESTHOOD

I. The Old Testament Background

There are several reasons why it is appropriate to begin our discussion with the concept of priesthood in the OT. First, when we come to the NT, we shall see that the term "priest" is not applied specifically to any Christian. Therefore, if we wish to relate our Catholic priesthood to what the Bible actually denominates as priesthood, it is to the OT we must turn. If one objects that the Christian priesthood is more directly related to the priesthood of Jesus himself, one must recognize that, particularly as explained in the Epistle to the Hebrews, Jesus' priesthood must be understood against the background of the OT. Second, through a misunderstanding, the Israelite concept of priesthood is being denigrated by some today. I have heard it argued that the original Christian idea of a specialized ministry was a simple one of service to others until at the end of the 1st century A.D. the theology of the ministry came under the influence of a revival of the OT notion of a sacrificial priesthood, a notion that eventually corrupted the Christian ideal of the ministry by creating a priestly caste set apart from others. I find this too simplified as regards the early history of the Christian ministry, and erroneous in its distorted picture of the

Israelite priesthood. If such ideas are widespread, a brief review[1] of OT priesthood will serve as a healthy corrective.

A. The Character of the Israelite Priesthood

We may begin by pointing out that at different times in the OT period the role of priest was filled in different ways. The patriarchs, as heads of families or tribal groups, performed what we would consider specifically priestly functions, such as offering sacrifice (Gen 22:2; 31:54). In later times, corresponding to growth in the social organization of Israel, there emerged an office of priesthood, and some men devoted all or a good deal of their time to being priests. Since priestly functions demanded both knowledge and skill, a priestly professionalism developed, especially in connection with the tribe of Levi. (Levi may originally have been a secular tribe that survived a loss of territory by specializing in cult. This is reflected in the idealized tradition that Levi had no share in the Promised Land, for the Lord was its portion.) We see this development illustrated in the story of Micah in Jgs 17: Micah built his own shrine and made one of his sons a priest; but when the opportunity came to have a Levite as priest, Micah gladly seized upon it. The professionalism of the tribe of Levi resulted eventually in an exclusively levitical priesthood.[2]

This history has some interesting implications for the Christian priesthood. We note in the OT the adaptability of priesthood—a fact that prepares us for much adaptation in the development and history of the Christian priesthood. The

---

[1] The various biblical encyclopedias and dictionaries offer detailed information on the OT priesthood. Particularly useful is R. de Vaux, *Ancient Israel* (New York: McGraw Hill, 1961), pp. 345-57.

[2] The later history of the Levites is not of particular concern here. Briefly, the levitical priests of the shrines outside Jerusalem, particularly those of the Northern Kingdom, were treated as inferior and not allowed to offer sacrifice at the Jerusalem Temple. Eventually they came to be known as "Levites," constituting a clergy of inferior rank and function, distinct from "priests."

emergence of a professional priesthood is also noteworthy. In Israelite theology the whole people was worthy of the title "kingdom of priests, holy nation" (Exod 19:6), but that did not in any way prevent or conflict with the development of a specialized priesthood. (We shall return to this important point when we discuss the NT priesthood.) This specialized priesthood in the OT was not a vocation or a charism in the modern sense of the terms. The prophet, the judge, and the king were the recipients of a charism, for they were called and specially gifted by God. But the levitical priest was born into the priesthood; he could serve as a priest because by birth he was a member of a priestly tribe and family. His calling from God was only in terms of a divine providence guiding his birth, and it is precisely in that limited sense that we must understand the reference in Heb 5:1, 4 to the "high priest chosen from among men ... who does not take the honor upon himself but is *called* by God." While the concept of birth into the priesthood is foreign to the Catholic understanding of priestly vocation, we can still learn something from it. If the Christian priesthood is entered through personal, voluntary acceptance, it remains an office for which one must have skill and training. Just as among the Levites priestly lore was taught to the members of the tribe, so the Church demands a long period of intellectual and spiritual formation before one can become a priest. "Professionalism" is an objectionable term if it conveys the idea of technical proficiency that lacks warmth and personal interest, but it is not an unworthy characteristic of the priesthood if it conveys the idea of skill and training needed to do a job well. Too charismatic an understanding of the Christian ministry is just as dangerous as too professional an understanding of it. Perhaps one of the most practical objections to a new type of priesthood whereby men could serve as priests for a few years and then leave would be the serious lack of professionalism that would inevitably result from such frequent change-overs. As a side light on this same problem of professionalism in the priesthood one may reflect on the infrequency of the term "churchman" in reference to priests today. Some object to the term because they find in it the implication that the priest is more a member of the Church than a layman. But that is not the real connotation of "church-man"; rather it refers to one who devotes all his time to the Church's work. It contains within it an element of healthy pro-fessionalism that serves to prevent the specialized ministry from losing its identity. The failure to use it frequently today may be symptomatic of a one-sidedly charismatic appreciation of ministry.

The levitical priesthood, although it was not a vocation in our sense, did not lack an ideal of sanctity. The priest was sanctified for and by his work; he had to be holy in order to handle the things that belonged to God. If the whole nation was under the command, "You shall be holy, for I the Lord your God am holy" (Lev 19:2), a special holiness was demanded of the priest because he served God in a special way. God instructed Moses, "You shall consecrate him, for he presents the bread of your God; he shall be holy to you, for I the Lord who sanctify you am holy" (Lev 21:8). Since the holiness of God Himself is connected with His being apart, a major aspect of the holiness of the priest consisted of his separation from the secular or profane. Greater purity was demanded of him in his general contacts with society, but the demand for purity and non-con-tamination was especially stringent during the time when he exercised priestly service at the sanctuary. The priest had to wash himself and wear special garments when he took part in sacrifice, so that it would be clear that he had removed himself from the contamination of the everyday.

In the history of priestly spirituality the Church may have taken over too simply the OT ideal of the holy purity of priests, for there has been a heavy emphasis on the priest as a man apart. An exclusive concentration on the holiness of separation does not do justice to the fact that the Christian priest is heir to the apostles who were sent into the whole world. Yet today, after Vatican II and the constitution on "The Church in the Modern World" (*Gaudium et spes*), it is the opposite mentality that is dominant. The distinction between the holy and the pro-fane is no longer popular, and the cry is for a Christianity that informs the secular world and is very much a part of that world. Nothing is more likely to "turn off" the modern aspirant to the priesthood than talk of the priest as a man apart. Precisely in this clime the OT can serve as a challenge and a corrective. Heaven forbid that we try to reinstate the overemphasis on the holiness of separation, but just as great a monstrosity can be made of the priest by a myopic concentration on the holiness of secularization. A God who is not holier than the world is otiose; and similarly a priesthood that does not stand apart in some way is a priesthood that is not needed. The least that one can ask of a specialized ministry is that it be special. The priestly ordination ritual of the Roman Catholic Church has traditionally contained the words: *Agnoscite quod agitis; imitamini quod tractatis*—"Understand what you do; imitate what you handle." This is a healthy echo of the OT demand for special holiness from priests because of the task that is theirs (so long as we remember that the special type of holiness dictated by task is not necessarily greater holiness). Perhaps it is worth noting that the holiness of separation demanded of Israelite priests did not make religion at all remote from the lives of the people; in its own way Israel exemplified a better harmony of religion and the world (admittedly anachronistic terms for the OT) than has been found in the Church.

With a certain amusement we may report that the OT ideal of the priesthood was not entirely idealistic. If a man was born into the priestly tribe, he still had to be installed in the priestly office. Over the centuries this was done in several ways, but the oldest seems to have involved "the filling of his hands" (Exod 32:29). Presumably this referred to putting into his hands some of the revenues that he had a right to, as an installment at the beginning of his ministry (Jgs 17:10; 18:4). (While we heartily praise reforms within Catholicism about stipends in order to erase once and for all the image of a priest as a man with his hand out, it may be of some comfort to reflect on the antiquity of the image.) And so if Israelite theology demanded of priests a holiness of separation, it was eminently practical about the priests' need for support. It is curious that our times, which are so insistent on plunging the priest into the secular, seem to be becoming less practical about the needs of religion for money.

B. The Functions of the Israelite Priesthood

In Deut 33:8-10 we have a poetic description of the three basic functions of the Israelite priesthood, seemingly arranged in order of importance.

(1) At a sanctuary the priests *consulted the Urim and Thummim,* i.e., the sacred lots that were cast in order to discover God's answer to a problem that had been posed (I Sam 14:41-42). The Israelites went to the sanctuary "to consult Yahweh" and to find His will, and the priest was instrumental in answering their request. This priestly function seems to have gone into gradual decline during the period of the monarchy, as the prophet took over the task of disclosing God's will to Israel. By the time of the Second Temple (after the Babylonian Exile) the role of the priest as the one who answered in God's name seems to have died out altogether; this is hinted in Ezra 2:63 (Neh 7:65) which speaks of waiting "until a priest with Urim and Thummim should arise." Today we judge as somewhat superstitious the manner in which the Israelite priest consulted God's will, but it is important to note that the OT concept of priesthood once embraced the function of proclaiming God's will to men. The incorporation of that function into the Christian priesthood was, therefore, not simply a matter of grafting onto priesthood an element that was foreign to it.

(2) Another function of the levitical priest mentioned in Deut 33:10 is *teaching:* "They shall teach Jacob your ordinances, and Israel your Law." The Torah or Law of God was in the hands of the priest to communicate to men (Jer 18:18; Mal 2:6). It was the priests of the Northern Kingdom, probably at the shrine of Shechem, who preserved, enlarged, and assembled the magnificent collection of laws that we now find in Deut 12—26, while the priests of the Southern Kingdom gave us the "Priestly Collection" of laws, found in Lev 1—16, Exod 25—31, and Num 1—10. Unfortunately, to mention religious law today is to raise the specter of a formalized and spiritless desiccation of religion—a reaction that results from an overdose of legalism within our Catholic tradition, and perhaps from an

uncritical examination of Paul's attitude toward law.[3] But if one
reads the warm and vibrant presentation in Deuteronomy where
law is the heart of a persuasive religious exhortation, one sees
how noble was the priestly teaching of law. The priests were
inculcating a way of life—not an external, impersonal norm but
an interiorized principle of spirituality. "This command which
I enjoin on you today is neither too hard nor too remote for you.
It is not way up in heaven . . . nor is it across the sea . . . it is
something that is very near to you, right on your lips and in
your heart, so that you have only to keep it" (Deut 30:11-14).
When we recall the scope of Israelite law, reaching into every
corner of life, we realize to what an extent the priests were the
ones who formed Israel by their teaching. Once again, in a later
period the priests lost this teaching function to the scribes, but
that should not blind us to the comprehensiveness of the earlier
OT concept of priesthood, a concept wherein the first two functions we have discussed were oriented from God to man.

Judaism today has not lost the sense of the sacred character
of the teaching function; the honorific title of the Jewish religious leader is "Rabbi," which is the same title of "Teacher"
given by the disciples to Jesus in John 1:38. Recently in a con-
versation with a well-known rabbi, I mentioned that some of
the Catholic religious orders whose primary work was teaching
were undergoing a vocation crisis, because the young aspirants
were questioning whether teaching was a proper full-time task
for a priest. The rabbi literally became white and exclaimed,
"Have you Christians lost to such an extent your roots in
Judaism? Have you forgotten that a man who teaches is per-
forming one of the most sacred of all functions, one that brings

---

[3] Paul is waging a polemic against those Jewish Christians who
insist on Gentile Christian acceptance of the Law, and his statements about the impotence of the Law have to be interpreted in
light of that polemic. But even with this allowance, Paul seems
defective in his appreciation of the covenant aspect of the Law.
Christians must remember that there are other voices in the NT
that are much more positive toward the Law, including seemingly
the voice of Jesus himself. Matthew's attitude is very unlike Paul's:
"Not the smallest letter of the Law, not even the smallest part of a
letter, will be done away with until it all comes true" (Matt 5:18).

him close to God Himself?" I could but hear in his words a
distant echo of that unknown prophet whose book is the last in
the collection of the prophets, a prophet who castigated priests
because they had lost the vision of their vocation: "Teaching is
to be sought from the mouth of the priest, for he is the mes-
senger of the Lord of Hosts; but you have turned away from
that course" (Mal 2:7-8). With partial justification some will
suggest a distinction between a Catholic priest's teaching of
purely secular subjects and his (more appropriate) teaching of
religion or subjects capable of religious orientation. Yet it is
worthy of reflection that the Hebrews drew no such sharp distinction within the wisdom given by God to men (cf. I Kings
4:29-34).

(3) The last of the priestly functions mentioned in Deut
33:10 is that of *sacrifice and cultic offering*.[4] Because the first
and second functions of the OT priesthood were shifted over to
the prophet and the scribe respectively, sacrifice was the principal function left to the priest at the end of the OT period. And
so we Christians, who often know the OT only through the NT,
have tended to think of the levitical priesthood simply as a
sacrificial priesthood. We have not recognized the narrowness
in the description of the Israelite priesthood given in Heb 5:1
which says that a priest "is appointed to act on behalf of men
in relation to God, to offer gifts and sacrifices for sins." Much
of the priestly activity in early OT times was in the opposite
direction, from God to men, as seen in the first two functions we
discussed. The common denominator of the three functions is
that the priest was an intermediary between God and men, the

---

[4] Perhaps a note about bloody sacrifice would not be amiss if we
are to correct a common misunderstanding. In the OT the sacrificial function of the priest was not identified with the killing or
immolation of the animal victim, for the victim was normally im-
molated by the person who brought it. The priest was properly
involved in the part of the sacrificial action that focused on the
victim's blood, which was to touch the altar sacred to God, and on
sections of the animal that were to be placed on the altar. Thus, as
R. de Vaux, *Ancient Israel*, p. 356, remarks, the priest was in a
very real sense "the minister of the altar," a still-current Christian
expression.

bridge uniting them in a two-way interchange. This is still an ideal for the Christian priesthood.

II. The New Testament Background

A. The Absence of Christian Priests in the NT

When we move from the OT to the NT, it is striking that while there are pagan priests and Jewish priests on the scene, no individual Christian is ever specifically identified as a priest.[5] The Epistle to the Hebrews speaks of the high priesthood of Jesus by comparing his death and entry into heaven with the actions of the Jewish high priest who went into the Holy of Holies in the Tabernacle once a year with a blood offering for himself and for the sins of his people (Heb 9:6-7). But it is noteworthy that the author of Hebrews does not associate the priesthood of Jesus with the Eucharist or the Last Supper; neither does he suggest that other Christians are priests in the likeness of Jesus.

In fact, the once-for-all atmosphere that surrounds the priesthood of Jesus in Hebrews (10:12-14) has been offered as an explanation of why there are no Christian priests in the NT period. Hans Küng, after commenting on Hebrews, says, "The significance of these ideas for the New Testament is that all human priesthood has been fulfilled and finished. . . ."[6] How-

---

[5] This fact is obscured in some NT translations which render the term *presbyteros* ("presbyter, elder") as "priest." This word should be kept as a translation for the technical term *hiereus* (Latin *sacerdos*).

[6] H. Küng, *The Church* (New York: Sheed and Ward, 1967), p. 366. While there is much that is admirable in Küng's book, I have many exegetical criticisms of his treatment of the special Christian ministry. Since I cannot enter into a detailed discussion of the book in this type of monograph, the reader would be well advised to read M. M. Bourke, "Reflections on Church Order in the New Testament," *Catholic Biblical Quarterly* 30 (1968), pp. 493-511; and Y. Congar, "*L'Église* de Hans Küng," *Revue des Sciences Philosophiques et Théologiques* 53 (1969), pp. 693-706.

ever, I find it quite illegitimate to generalize from Hebrews to the whole NT situation. With most critical scholars, we should probably date Hebrews to the period after the destruction of the Temple when the sacrificial functioning of the Jewish priesthood had ceased. The author works that event into a theological interpretation by claiming that Jesus is a priest who has replaced the priests and sacrifices of Israel. While he is not the only late author of the NT to hold this view (there are elements of a similar mentality in the Fourth Gospel), one is hard pressed to find either the theology of the priesthood of Jesus or such a strong theology of replacement in the earlier NT writings. In fact, one may doubt that the theology of Hebrews had much influence even in the late NT period; for, as we shall see, shortly after Hebrews was written we begin to find in the sub-apostolic literature our first instances of the term "priest" and of the imagery of priesthood being applied to the Christian ministry.

Another explanation for the silence of the NT about Christian priests is one made popular by Luther and now receiving some approbation in Catholic circles, namely, that all Christians were looked on as priests and so there was no need for special priests. The scriptural basis for this contention is the fact that the classic "kingdom of priests" text, Exod 19:6, found an echo in the NT. For instance, I Pet 2:9 addresses a Christian audience: "You are a chosen race, a royal priesthood, a holy nation, God's own people" (see also Rev 1:6; 5:10; 20:6). However, recently J. H. Elliott, a Lutheran scholar, has subjected the so-called universal priesthood text of I Peter to a detailed examination,[7] and his conclusions are a rather startling rejection of Luther's interpretation. Elliott maintains that "kingdom of priests" is to be understood of Christians much in the same way as it was understood of Israel in Exod 19:6—because this is a people bound to God by a special covenant relationship, it is to be a specially holy people, nay, holy as priests. In other words, the text does not primarily concern priestly function (in particular, cultic sacrifice) but priestly holiness. He points out that

---

[7] J. H. Elliott, *The Elect and the Holy* (Supplements to Novum Testamentum XII; Leiden: Brill, 1966).

the idea of the royal priesthood of the people of Israel in the
OT did not prevent the emergence of the cultic levitical priesthood, and so one cannot argue from the royal priesthood of
Christians against the existence of a Christian specialized cultic
priesthood. Moreover, the idea of a universal Christian priesthood is never connected in the NT in any way with the Eucharist. The statement in I Pet 2:5 that Christians offer "spiritual
sacrifices" is a figurative reference to a holy way of life. Elliott
cites with approval the dictum of Y. Congar, "Nowhere in the
New Testament is there any reference to the worship and priesthood of the faithful *in the Eucharist or even in the sacraments
. . . or in the Church's public worship."*[8]

---

[8] Y. Congar, *Lay People in the Church* (Westminster, Md.:
Newman, 1957), p. 126; italics mine. Some readers may object to
these remarks about the priesthood of the faithful on the grounds
of Vatican II: "For their part, the faithful join in the offering of
the Eucharist by virtue of their royal priesthood" (*Lumen Gentium*,
10). I have no wish to lessen the role of laity; indeed, a revival of
emphasis on the laity is one of the most healthy features in contemporary Catholicism. Nor do I challenge the assertion that the
laity join in the offering of the Eucharist; but I do question any
contention that this offering of the Eucharist is in virtue of the fact
that *according to the NT* Christians are a royal priesthood. It is a
bit curious that some who are perfectly willing to point out the
scholarly limitations of statements made at the Council of Trent
are indignant when similar limitations are pointed out in the documents of Vatican II (unless the limitations are on the conservative
end of the spectrum). While the Fathers of Vatican II responded
well to modern biblical insights, many statements in the documents
are biblically naive, as we shall see when we discuss the bishops as
successors of the apostles. I suspect that since priesthood and
Eucharist went together in the minds of many Vatican Council II
theologians and Fathers, they simply assumed a relationship between the biblical term "royal priesthood" and the Eucharist. Perhaps there is some justification in the history of theology for
attaching the offering of the Eucharist to the idea of the priesthood
of the faithful—I have not investigated the problem—but I agree
with Elliott that there is no proof that the NT authors made this
association. In a similar vein of criticism, I find the section entitled
"The Priesthood of All Believers" in H. Küng's *The Church*,
pp. 363-87, somewhat unsatisfactory because, while, drawing on the
NT, he rightly speaks of the power of all Christians to baptize, to

A more traditional Catholic explanation of why individual Christians are not specifically designated as priests in the NT is that the apostles who presided at the Eucharist were priests in everything but name, for the name was too closely associated with the Jewish priests of the Temple. But this explanation is based on a serious oversimplification about apostles in the NT, as we shall see in Chapter Two, and suffers from the added difficulty of unwarrantedly supposing that in NT times the Eucharist was thought of as a sacrifice and therefore associated with priesthood. Because of the origins of Christianity in Judaism we would really have to suppose just the opposite: animal sacrifice would be thought of in terms of blood and there was no visible blood in the Eucharist. True, there are sacrificial overtones in the traditional eucharistic words of Jesus (the mention of the shedding of blood, the covenant motif, the "for you" theme), but this coloring was understandable because Jesus spoke these words before his bloody death. There is no proof that the Christian communities who broke the eucharistic bread after the resurrection would have thought that they were offering sacrifice. In these observations I am not questioning the legitimacy of the development in later theology whereby the Church came to understand the Eucharist as a sacrifice; indeed a recent study by a Calvinist argues that there was real continuity in such a development and that it is loyal to the *implications* of the NT.[9] I am simply pointing out that such a theology was a post-NT development, and so we have no basis for assuming that early Christians would have considered as a priest the one who presided at the eucharistic meal.

Yet the traditional explanation of the silence of the NT about Christian priests has one point that may supply the key to a much more radical solution, namely, the failure to use the name "priest" because it was associated with the Jewish priests in the Temple. I think more was involved than an association of

take part in the Lord's Supper, etc., he does so under the rubric of priesthood. Is there any evidence in the NT that such functions would be seen as priestly?

[9] J. de Watteville, *Le sacrifice dans les textes eucharistiques des premiers siècles* (Paris: Delachaux et Niestlé, 1966).

the name with the Jewish priesthood; rather I suggest that the early Christians acknowledged the Jewish priesthood as valid and therefore never thought of a priesthood of their own. Many of our assumptions about the early Christian community flow from the erroneous supposition that Christianity was thought of as a new religion with its own religious institutions. But our best evidence is exactly to the contrary: at the beginning Christians constituted a movement within Judaism, differing only in some features (especially in the belief that Jesus was the Messiah, that with him God had inaugurated the eschatological times, and that therefore Gentiles could now participate fully in the blessings of Israel without formally adopting all the precepts of the Law of Moses). The Christians understood themselves as the renewed Israel, not immediately as the new Israel;[10] and they expected that soon all the children of Israel would join this renewal movement. The Book of Acts (2:46) reports that while they broke (eucharistic?) bread in their homes, the Jerusalem Christians kept up their daily attendance at the Temple—certainly no sign of a break with the Jerusalem priesthood. Even Paul, who insisted that Gentile Christians were not bound by the Law, is still presented in Acts 21:26 as going to the Temple for offerings as late as the year 58.

For the emergence of the idea of a special Christian priesthood in place of the Jewish priesthood several major changes of direction had to intervene. *First,* Christians had to come to think of themselves as constituting a new religion distinct from Judaism and replacing the Jews of the Synagogue as God's covenanted people. Some Christians may have been (unwittingly?) moving in this direction from a very early period, e.g., the "left-wing" group called Hellenists in Acts 6:1, if we can judge their theology from the words of Stephen, a Hellenist leader, who attacks the Temple in Acts 7:47-50. But this was scarcely the dominant Christian view before 70. After that date

---

[10] Not in the New Testament but in the *Epistle of Barnabas* 5:7 do we find the first explicit mention of Christians as "the new people." The difference between "new" and "renewed" is significant, for "renewed" does not imply a counterpart of "old" in the sense of defunct or displaced.

a combination of factors separated Christianity from Judaism:
(a) numerically Gentiles became more and more dominant in
the Church; (b) the Jerusalem community, which was more
inclined to be Jewish in outlook, lost leadership to Rome and
other major centers, like Antioch, Ephesus, and Alexandria;
(c) the Temple was destroyed, and this was interpreted by
Christians as God's final rejection of the Jews because of their
failure to accept Jesus; (d) Judaism, fighting for its own existence, became more narrow; and in the period between 85 and
90 the synagogues began excommunicating the Jewish sectarians, including the Christians. It is precisely in this era that we
would situate the author of Hebrews, as discussed above. The
insistence of this author that Jesus was a royal priest[11] who by
his death rendered otiose the continuation of sacrifice is a form
of the claim that Christianity has replaced the old Israel. Another form is the Johannine assertion that the Temple has been
replaced by Jesus' body (John 2:20-21) and that the major
Jewish feasts have lost their significance in face of God's gifts
through Jesus.[12]

But there still had to be a *second* development before the
emergence of the concept of a special Christian priesthood:
Christianity had to have a sacrifice at which a priesthood could

---

[11] In Catholic circles a rather confused mystique has been built
around the royal priesthood of Jesus "according to the order of
Melchizedek" (Heb 5:10). Historically the expression in Ps 110:4
may reflect an honorific title claimed by the Davidic monarch in
Jerusalem, associating his royal line with that of the much older
pagan priest-kings of that city (see Gen 14:18). The author of
Hebrews fastened upon the expression as a scriptural way of defending (a) the designation of Jesus as a priest although he was not
born of the levitical tribe—Melchizedek was a priest although he
was not given a priestly genealogy; (b) the claim that Jesus was
both a priest and the Davidic Messiah—the title of "priest according to the order of Melchizedek" had been used by the Davidic
kings.

[12] John 5—10 is a section organized around a series of feasts
(Sabbath, Passover, Tabernacles, Dedication), and on each occasion
Jesus' claims for himself reflect on the motif of the feast. See R. E.
Brown, *The Gospel according to John* (Anchor Bible 29; Garden
City, N. Y.: Doubleday, 1966), pp. 201-4.

,preside. This second condition was fulfilled when the Eucharist was seen as an unbloody sacrifice replacing the bloody sacrifices no longer offered in the now-destroyed Temple. This attitude appears in Christian writings about the end of the 1st century or the beginning of the 2nd. *Didache* 14 instructs Christians: "Assemble on the Lord's Day, breaking bread and celebrating the Eucharist; but first confess your sins that your *sacrifice* [*thysia*] may be a pure one. . . . For it was of this that the Lord spoke, 'Everywhere and always offer me a pure sacrifice.' " The citation is from Mal 1:10-11, a passage which became a very important factor in the Christian understanding of the Eucharist. As Christians read the words of the prophet, the Eucharist seemed to fulfill Malachi's prediction of a pure sacrifice offered among the Gentiles from the rising of the sun until its setting, as contrasted with the sacrifice that God said He would no longer accept from the hands of the Jewish priests. It is noteworthy that besides speaking of the Eucharist in a sacrificial context, *Didache* 13:3 says that the charismatic prophets are the Christian "high priests"; an earlier passage would seem to indicate that such prophets were allowed to celebrate the Eucharist (10:7—although some scholars think that the reference is to the *agapē* meal). At about the same time, in his plea that Christian liturgical offerings and services should be structured, Clement of Rome (*I Clem* 40) calls on the analogy of the OT structure of high priest, priests, and levites. Thus the Christian terminology of eucharistic sacrifice and of priesthood begin to be used side by side, frequently contrasted with their rejected Jewish counterparts. Just after the end of the 2nd century Tertullian (*De Baptismo* 17) can speak of the bishop as the *summus sacerdos* and Hippolytus of Rome (*Apostolic Tradition* III 5) can refer to the "high priestly spirit" of the bishop.

Such a picture of the development of the Christian priesthood must of necessity modify our understanding of the claim that historically Jesus instituted the priesthood at the Last Supper. This statement is true to the same real but nuanced extent as the statement that the historical Jesus instituted the Church. By selecting followers to take part in the proclamation of God's kingdom, Jesus formed the nucleus of what would develop into a community and ultimately into the Church. By giving special significance to the elements of the (Passover?) meal that he ate with his disciples on the night before he died, Jesus supplied his followers with a community rite that would ultimately be seen as a sacrifice and whose celebrants would hence be understood as priests.

In summary, however, the fact that in NT times those who presided at the Eucharist were not necessarily considered priests does not mean that the NT has nothing to teach us about priesthood. The role of presiding at the Eucharist, however it was filled and whatever the functionary was called, did exist in the NT Church, even though it was but one of many special ministries, some of which are far more prominent in the pages of Scripture. The fact that we cannot so simply associate priesthood with the Last Supper context and that we have to understand it as an evolving concept opens us to the understanding that when the Christian priesthood did emerge, it represented more than the heritage of presiding at the Eucharist. The priesthood represents the combination or distillation of several distinct roles and special ministries in the NT Church.[13] And, in fact, some of those other roles and ministries that funneled into the formal priesthood (as it emerged somewhere in the course of the 2nd century) have colored the basic understanding of what a priest should be more than have the task of celebrating the eucharistic sacrifice and the OT background with which that task was associated.

---

[13] There is a difference of theological emphasis in the fact that Catholics speak of their clergy as "priests," while many Protestants speak of their clergy as "ministers," although in part the difference stems from the Protestant preference for NT terminology. One can minister to or serve a congregation without necessarily presiding at the Eucharist, and one can be a priest who offers the eucharistic sacrifice without necessarily serving the needs of the congregation in any other way. De facto, however, the duties performed by the two types of clergy are often quite similar; and the fact that the priest does more than preside at the Eucharist is a practical proof of our thesis that the priesthood is heir to a multiplicity of roles and ministries.

B. The NT Antecedents of Priestly Ministry

Let us now consider in detail four principal roles or ministries in the NT that ultimately funneled into the Christian priesthood, namely, the disciple, the apostle, the presbyter-bishop,
and the celebrant of the Eucharist (the last briefly because of
the discussion above). These are not the only antecedents of
the priesthood that might be discussed, but they are the most
obvious and will supply the thoughtful reader with a methodo-
logical approach applicable to other antecedents that may occur
to him.

1. *The Disciple*

The spiritual idealism of the later Christian priesthood was
dominantly shaped by the role of the disciple of Jesus as graph-
ically portrayed in the Gospels.[14] In a very real sense all Christians are called to be disciples of Jesus, but it has been felt that
those engaged in the special Christian ministry are bound in a
special way by the demands of Christian discipleship. The fact
that Jesus chose from among his followers Twelve[15] to be with

---

[14] See K. H. Schelkle, *Discipleship and Priesthood* (New York:
Herder and Herder, 1965). Undoubtedly, in reference to discipleship as in other matters, the Gospels represent a development
beyond the purely historical. While I shall try here not to violate
the cautions imposed by biblical criticism, we should remember
that what has played the formative role in the history of the priesthood has been precisely the *Gospel* ideal of discipleship. Some may
wonder whether discipleship necessarily had to have this formative
role as regards priesthood; but here as elsewhere I deal with what
has happened, not with what might have happened.

[15] In Chapter Two we shall treat the Twelve as apostles (and in
distinction from other apostles), but here we are concerned with
the Twelve as disciples during the ministry—apostleship is a post-
resurrectional concept. The evidence that the Twelve existed as a
group during the ministry is persuasive in my judgment. The
Qumran (Dead Sea) Scrolls show that a grouping of twelve (in
imitation of the twelve patriarchs who were the eponymous an-
cestors of the twelve tribes) was very much alive in Jewish eschatological thought.

him more intimately set up a pattern wherein Christians designated to the special ministry have been thought to be obliged to
the closer discipleship of the Twelve. In brief, if Christians are
called upon to be a light to the world, it has been thought that
priests are called upon to be a light to the Christian community.

When we examine the NT portrait of discipleship, we find
it a very Jewish picture. The Rabbi has his pupils gathered
around him in order to be close to him, to see what he does,
and to live like him so that they may represent him to others.
There is an intimacy that almost breaks the bonds of superior
and inferior relationship: "You are my friends . . . no longer do
I call you servants" (John 15:14-15). Yet it remains clear who
is the source of the influence: "A disciple is not above his
teacher" (Matt 10:24).

What is particularly significant for the subsequent development of the Christian priesthood is the element of vocation in
discipleship. We have said that the OT priesthood came by
birth; but because Christian priests are also disciples, they accept a calling as did the companions of Jesus. The radical or
absolute quality of this call has deeply marked the idealism of
the Christian ministry. For the disciple there can be only one
master, Jesus. If he seeks to serve another master, he falls under
the injunction of the parabolic saying, "No man can serve two
masters . . ." (Matt 6:24). When the call comes, the would-be
disciple cannot temporize, no matter how noble his reason, but
must accept wholeheartedly. Jesus reacts harshly to the man
who is called but seeks first to satisfy the sacred duty of burying
his father. "Follow me," is Jesus' command, "and let the dead
bury their own dead" (Matt 8:21-22). In a Jewish setting such
an outrageous order means that nothing, no matter how sacred,
can interfere with one's response to the call of discipleship, for
this is an invitation issued in the name of the kingdom or rule
of God. Nor, when one has begun to follow as a disciple, is
there any turning back: "No one who has put his hand to the
plow and looks back is fit for the kingdom of God" (Luke
9:62). As the NT presents the ideal of discipleship, it is almost
a monomaniacally consuming vocation, occupying all the interest of the disciple and allowing no competitive diversion what-

soever: "If any one comes to me and does not hate his own father and mother and wife and children and brothers and sisters, yes, and even his own life, he cannot be my disciple" (Luke 14:26).[16]

We should consider the practical implications that such a lofty ideal of vocation has had for the Christian priesthood, since priests have been expected to meet the most rigorous demands of discipleship. For instance, the ideal has strongly militated against a part-time or temporary priesthood. It is true, of course, that in missionary circumstances priests have engaged in paid secular work to support themselves, but Catholics have traditionally understood such work as subservient to the priestly ministry. We have not countenanced the idea that priesthood was a part-time task that could be dealt with in the spare time permitted by another occupation. Perhaps today, because of the shortage of clergy, we may have to ordain men who are engaged full time in other tasks and devote only one day a week to a priestly function (e.g., celebrating Mass on Sunday). But the strength of the Gospel ideal of vocation suggests that such an approach will be considered an exception to the rule of a full-time priesthood. Similarly the NT portrait of the vocation of the disciples has guided the Church away from the concept of a temporary priesthood, in the sense of a man's being ordained for a fixed period of time and thus limiting his commitment. Priesthood has been conceived precisely in terms of a lifetime vocation with no turning back, and the laicizing of priests has been counted a concession to human weakness. I realize that in the present climate I am treading here on very sensitive ground; but at least those who advocate easy laicization should consider that more is at stake than the revocation of medieval canon law —this problem touches upon the heart of discipleship as presented in the Gospels. If it is objected that the NT words are directed to all Christians and refer to no turning back from the acceptance of God's rule (kingdom), *I would agree wholeheartedly*. But we cannot read the Gospels in a way that would

---

[16] "Hate" is hyperbole, and really a question of preference is involved; but the dramatic force of the language is indicative of the intensity of adherence to Jesus demanded by discipleship.

water down the specific fidelity and generosity required of those chosen from the wider group of followers to be Jesus' special disciples so that they may worthily represent him to others. In short we cannot discount the *a fortiori* implications of the discipleship of the Twelve for the *ideals* of the priesthood.

We speak frequently today about hardships as a modifying factor in the Church's understanding of the lifetime nature of priestly vocation. Legitimate as that may be (and who wishes to question the mercy of the Church), one must recognize that in the Gospels the vocation to special discipleship is portrayed precisely as a vocation to hardships too severe to be generally acceptable. The call of individual members of the Twelve ends on the theme of their leaving possessions and family to follow Jesus (Matt 4:22). Indeed, the disciples characterize themselves as men who have left everything for Jesus (Matt 19:27). In the story of the young man who has lived a virtuous life, the point of decision as to whether he will follow Jesus is his willingness to give up all his possessions (Matt 19:16-22). To the scribe who wishes to join the other disciples, Jesus says, "Foxes have dens, and birds of the air have nests, but the Son of Man has nowhere to lay his head" (Matt 8:19-20). In other words (unlike well-intentioned advisers who rhapsodize to prospective seminarians about the attractiveness of the priestly life), Jesus confronts the candidate to discipleship with a stark portrait of the hardships involved. If the Gospels define even the general following of Jesus in terms of self-denial and of taking up the cross (Matt 10:38; 16:24, and parallels), they have to some extent foreclosed an understanding of the special ministry in which lifetime perseverance will be expected only of those who do not find hardships in the life. Discipleship involves patterning oneself on a master, and in this case the master is one whose own vocation came to its ultimate expression in suffering.

The ideals implicit in the NT portrait of the discipleship of the Twelve have had other implications for the priesthood besides that of the permanency of the ministry. Criticism of wealth and leisure as scandalous in the priesthood has sprung from an understanding that priests should live by the standards of discipleship. Today there is much criticism about the extent to which priests have become different from other Christians, especially where the difference consists in priests receiving more honor and more consideration than others. Again this type of distinction runs contrary to NT ideals, for the priest is supposed to be a disciple to him who came not to be ministered to but to minister (Matt 20:28), a master for whom it was anathema to have his disciples seeking first place (Mark 9:35). The campaign against priestly distinctions begins to run contrary to the Gospel only when the priest does not want to have anything more or different expected of him than is expected of other Christians. The argument that we should not expect too much because the priest is a man like other men conflicts with the challenging ideal of the discipleship of the Twelve.

The fact that the Western Catholic Church has demanded celibacy of its priests may also be seen as an application of the principle of discipleship. Of course, the Church knows that in the NT celibacy was not *demanded* of all who followed Jesus or even of the Twelve, but it was held up as an ideal to those who were able to bear it (Matt 19:12; I Cor 7:7-9). Since this ideal was held up precisely for the sake of the kingdom of heaven, from a very early period[17] the Church has not deemed it illogical to seek candidates willing to live by the ideal of celibacy among those who want to devote themselves in a special way to promoting the kingdom of heaven. By the law that allows only a celibate clergy the Western Catholic Church has ensured a large-scale, public witness of the celibate life. I do not wish to enter

---

[17] Often the false impression is given that priestly celibacy is a medieval imposition. It is true that a law applicable to the *whole* Western Church stems from the Middle Ages—in 1123 Lateran Council I declared that clerics in major orders could not validly marry; similarly, married men living with their wives could not be ordained to major orders—but in certain areas of the West the custom of celibacy for priests can be documented back to *ca.* 300. Even in areas where there was a married clergy, generally marriage had to be contracted before ordination; it was very widespread that an ordained priest could not marry. The first law imposing celibacy appeared in Spain in 306, and the movement was so strong that the Council of Nicaea (325) debated the advisability of making celibacy compulsory for clergy.

here into the complicated and heated debate of whether the law should be continued; but I would contend that, precisely because the witness of celibacy is conspicuously lacking in many other Christian churches, the Roman Catholic Church has an ecumenical duty to the Gospel to continue to bear an *effective* witness on this score. Perhaps this would be possible without a law, but one must admit that it is the law of priestly celibacy that makes it clear that those who accept it are doing so for the sake of Christ and not simply because they prefer to be bachelors. *Some* of the forms of optional celibacy being proposed would soon lead to obscuring the vocational character of celibacy and would reduce it to a personal idiosyncrasy.

As one reflects on the challenges offered to the priesthood by the NT portrait of discipleship, one cannot but judge that these ideals have often been poorly met. If our present crisis about the priesthood underlines this, it will have been worth all the anguish. However, it is permissible to wonder whether we are now engaged in simply another of the priestly reform movements that have brought the Gospel ideals to the fore over and over again. To some, at least, it seems that more is being questioned than the success with which priests meet the ideals and that the ideals themselves are being doubted. In other words, the name of the game may be the relevancy of the Gospels—does a 1st-century ideal of discipleship have anything to say to a 20th-century man? I, for one, think that the Gospel challenge to discipleship is just as relevant today as it was in the 1st century because it touches on the very essence of the generosity demanded of men if they are to be open to God's rule or kingdom. If some of the Gospel demands, such as permanent commitment, seem very difficult to us today, I find no proof that they were not very difficult in the 1st century. Others may disagree about the continuing relevance of the specific Gospel ideals of discipleship. So be it—my main goal is to try to clarify what values are at stake.

2. The Apostle

If the NT picture of the disciple has greatly influenced the

spirituality of the priesthood, especially as regards the conformity of life style to the model of Christ, it is the role of the
apostle that has shaped the Christian understanding of the
priest's ministry for others. The disciples were called not only to
be with Jesus but also to represent him to others. The Gospels
hint at this in having the disciples sent forth during the ministry
(Mark 6:7ff.).[18] Yet the definitive sending forth that constituted
apostolate came after the resurrection. All the Gospels join the
role of the disciple to that of the apostle by having the Twelve
(or Eleven) disciples of the ministry receive the post-resurrectional apostolic command (Matt 28:19; Luke 24:47-48; John
20:21; Marcan Appendix 16:15). However, the NT is generally
silent about the apostolate of the Twelve (we shall discuss in
Chapter Two what Luke reports in Acts), and consequently the
paradigm for the apostle is a figure who was not a disciple of
Jesus during the ministry, namely, Paul, who is often simply
called "The Apostle." Even though Paul would certainly consider himself a disciple or follower of Jesus, the fact that he
was not one of the Twelve disciples helps us to show that to a
very real extent the disciple and the apostle are separate roles.
True, one could scarcely be an apostle without having many of
the ideals of the disciple; but one might have those ideals without engaging in the vigorous activity of the "Pauline apostle"—
something that explains why a very spiritual priest can still be
an ineffective minister of the Gospel to others.

If the keynote of discipleship is the close following of Jesus,
today that theme would not necessarily be the primary attraction
to priestly life. The keynote of apostleship is service, and this
would probably be more spontaneously appealing to the modern
aspirant to the priesthood. But even here one must be careful
not to read a modern set of values back into Scripture; for while
Paul certainly thinks of himself as a servant, his primary em-

---

[18] It is difficult to judge how much of the mission in Galilee is a
retrojection of the post-resurrectional apostolic mission. Certainly
Matt 10 (17-18) with its mention of persecution by synagogues,
governors, and kings has read subsequent history back into the
words of Jesus. Yet the basic idea of a limited mission during the
ministry of Jesus remains plausible.

phasis in apostleship is not service to others but *service to Jesus Christ*. It is refreshing to realize that, whatever the nature of the much-discussed malady with which Paul was afflicted (Gal 4:13-15; II Cor 12:7), it was not an identity crisis. He is a man who can say, "By the grace of God I am what I am" (I Cor 15:10); and what he is, is an apostle of Jesus Christ. The fact that in the opening of his letters he alternates between calling himself an apostle of Jesus Christ (Gal, I-II Cor, Col, Eph) and a servant of Jesus Christ (Philip, Rom) shows how he understands the service of his apostolate. Of course, the service that he renders to Jesus involves a service to others, but Christ is both the origin and goal of his apostolic service. He is an apostle because he has been sent by the risen Jesus; and in the Jewish notion of apostolate the one sent *(shalûaḥ, shaliaḥ)* represents the one who sends, carrying not only the sender's authority but even his presence to others. Thus, Paul as an apostle presents Jesus to men, not only by his preaching ("We preach not ourselves but Jesus Christ as Lord, with ourselves as your servants for Jesus' sake"—II Cor 4:5), but also by his life ("It is no longer I who live but Christ who lives in me"—Gal 2:20). It is in light of this that he can extend that most audacious invitation: "Christ Jesus has made me his own. . . . My brothers, be imitators of me" (Philip 3:12, 17). The goal of all this apostolic service that originates in Jesus Christ is to bring men to Jesus: "I have made myself a servant of all in order to win many over" (I Cor 9:19). The servant of Jesus Christ, in Paul's outlook, is merely a bridge: "What is Apollos? What is Paul? They are servants [*diakonoi*] through whom you have believed" (I Cor 3:5).

Once we have grasped the extent to which Jesus Christ, both as origin and goal, totally colors Paul's concept of apostolic service, then it becomes valid to stress just how much service Paul rendered *to others* in Jesus Christ. Today, when we speak of priestly service to others, beyond the sacrificial and sacramental spheres, we tend to think of preaching, of counseling, of consoling, of visiting, of social or economic help, and even simply of friendship. Paul's dedicated service included all that —no warmer or more concerned figure emerges from the pages of the NT. But his service was still broader and included aspects that often we do not think of in terms of service. In order to deepen our reflections on the priesthood in the light of the NT background, it seems better to skip the more obvious forms of service and to concentrate on the thought-provoking and less obvious services.

The service of ordinary work. Paul earned his own living while he was evangelizing Corinth lest he be a burden to his converts and they think that he was seeking their money instead of themselves ("I seek not what is yours but you"—II Cor 12:13-14). This example of work is scarcely held up as an absolute norm, even by Paul himself (I Cor 9:4-7), and we find the Jerusalem apostles having to make a choice between waiting on tables and preaching the word of God (Acts 6:2). Yet Paul's example reminds us that ordinary work is within the possible scope of the sacred ministry, not as a primary occupation, perhaps, but as an auxiliary. Today when, as mentioned above, there is a movement to end the distinctions between the priest and the laity, curiously there is a paradoxical reaction among priests against doing work "that anyone could be hired to do." That reaction is justified if most of a priest's time were thus taken away from the real needs of his people, but sometimes it reflects a dislike for drudgery. Paul knew that ordinary work brought him close to those whom he hoped to win over for Christ, and one may well suspect that even today people will not understand priests whose idea of their calling is so exclusively evangelistic that they find no place in it for ordinary work (which often has its share of drudgery).

The service of collecting money. It is startling to see how much attention is devoted in the Pauline letters to raising money. While Paul was quite sensitive about imposing on others for his own needs, he did not hesitate to beg in order to alleviate the poverty of the Jerusalem church. By pressing his Gentile Christians to give money for Jerusalem, he hoped to keep them conscious of their larger relationships and to bind them to the churches of God in Palestine. He hoped to teach the Gentile converts the Christian need of sharing. In short, as in most subsequent church drives for money, he had a good cause and

felt that a contribution was an aspect of charity. Precisely for
this reason he did not regard it beneath his dignity as an apostle
or extraneous to his apostolic ministry to come back again and
again to this mundane question when writing to his congrega-
tions. Those who complain that church pulpits are too often the
organs of monetary appeals are certainly right, but one has good
Pauline backing for questioning a semi-Gnostic attitude whereby
a man thinks it an insult to his priesthood that he has to ask for
money. This is an approach to ministry that is too other-worldly
for the NT.

The service of prayer. The first two forms of service that
we have discussed militate against too exalted a notion of service to others. On the other hand, there is another aspect of the
Pauline ministry that reflects an even more exalted notion of
service than that to which we are accustomed. With all the
references today to serving others, how many stop to think that
prayer is a service? The passage in II Cor 9:11-12 shows the
breadth of Paul's understanding of service. He encourages the
Corinthians to be generous in contributing to the collection for
Jerusalem, "for the rendering of this service [*leitourgia*] not only
supplies the needs of God's people but also overflows in a flood
of thanksgiving to God." Thus, service is related to the praise
of God (a truly liturgical approach, since the liturgy is ecclesiastical service). If the prayer of praise comes within the range
of service, so does the prayer of petition for others. We find
Paul, the servant of Jesus Christ, constantly praying for his
communities. Indeed, the first of his preserved words are: "We
give thanks always for you all, constantly mentioning you in
our prayers" (I Thess 1:2), and the theme recurs at the beginning of many of his letters (Philip 1:4; Rom 1:9; Philemon 4;
Col 1:3; Eph 1:16). The Church has tried to remain faithful
to the concept that the sacred ministry should render a service
of prayer by commanding that those in major orders pray the
Divine Office every day and that the pastor offer a certain
number of Masses for his people. The formal character of such
mandatory prayer is not overly appreciated today, but an ac-
tivist priesthood that does not frequently render to the people

the service of prayer would be even less biblical than a priesthood that has to be commanded to pray.

The service of suffering. Recently in a discussion about apostolicity between the Faith and Order Commission of the World Council of Churches and the Vatican Secretariat for Promoting Christian Unity the participants were trying to isolate the essential characteristics of the Pauline apostle. A Protestant confrère rather startled all of us by suggesting that suffering was 'one of the most distinctive features of Paul as an apostle. The truth of his observation did not strike home until the next time I taught the Pauline Epistles in class; then I noticed how often Paul resorts to his suffering as a sign of the truth of the apostolic service that he renders to his communities. If as an apostle Paul is to present Jesus to men, he can do this effectively because he bears Jesus' death pangs in his own body (II Cor 4:10). He is a man who finds no rest but is "afflicted at every turn, from struggles without and anxieties within" (II Cor 7:5). A priesthood that is patterned on the Pauline apostolate cannot hope to escape being a life full of pressures! Paul's external struggles consist of his sickness and of the persecutions he has suffered, as we hear in the catalogue of ills advanced by Paul as a proof that he is a real apostle (II Cor 11:23ff.).

But it is Paul's inner anguish that may be of more import to us today. We live in a time when priestly loneliness and the feeling of not being appreciated are mentioned most frequently as causes for leaving the ministry. What then are we to make of the most effective of the apostles who sees himself as a man "set apart for the Gospel of God" (Rom 1:1). Yes, *"set apart,"* with all the isolation that phrase implies: "For it seems to me that God has made us apostles the most abject of mankind . . . a spectacle to the world, to angels, and to men. We are fools for the sake of Christ, while you are sensible Christians. We are weak, while you are strong. We are in disgrace, while you are honored" (1 Cor 4:9-10). There is bitter irony in these words, but irony that reflects personal anguish—the anguish of a man who feels himself both unappreciated and humanly inadequate. Yet, with that magnificent sense of the inversion of values that comes from knowing God's will, Paul is not defeated by his weaknesses. Rather he comes to understand that weakness makes him all the more valuable a servant of Jesus Christ, for what is accomplished through him is clearly by God's grace and not by human strength: "The Lord said to me 'My grace is all you need, for my power is perfected in weakness.' Hence I boast of my weakness, and then the power of Christ will rest upon me" (II Cor 12:9). Paul gradually realizes that his conformity to the death and resurrection of Jesus is not simply a matter of baptism (Rom 6:3-5); it is a matter of day-by-day suffering: "While we live, we are always being given up to death for Jesus' sake, so that the life of Jesus may be manifested in our mortal flesh" (II Cor 4:11). Through such an apostolate of suffering the Gospel is advanced (Philip 1:12).

The service of correction. If, *prima facie,* service does not suggest prayer and suffering, the correction of others is even less likely to be included when one opts for a life of service. This is singularly true in an age where correction is thought of as unchristian, despite its presence in both Jesus' and Paul's preaching. Some of Paul's harshness stems from his own fiery character and is not of the essence of apostolic correction. He is scarcely offering us a model of interpersonal relationship when he addresses the Galatians as fools (Gal 3:1)—although one may wonder would he have been as effective if he were more diplomatic. Yet, leaving aside the outbursts of ire, one must still conclude from the Pauline letters that a good bit of his pastoral care consists in correcting abuses among Christians: abuses on a personal level (quarreling, uncharitableness, immorality); abuses on an ecclesiastical or communal level (divisions, lack of respect for the Eucharist); and abuses on a doctrinal level (inadequate appreciation of faith, inadequate christology). From the anguish that Paul expresses in Gal 4:20 and II Cor 12:20 we know that correction and the inevitable resentment that it produces were not easy for him. But his constant appeal to his apostolate in his letters of correction shows that for him it is a matter of apostolic duty and part of his service to Jesus Christ. "My children," he writes to the Galatians whom he has just called fools, "I am in travail with you again until Christ be formed in you" (Gal 4:19).

We all find distasteful the picture of the priest whose sermons consist largely of scoldings and "don'ts"—he soon makes a travesty of the mercy of Christ. But there is just as much a travesty in the priest who does not confront his people and challenge their standards, because he is unwilling to pay the price of losing his popularity. Today many priests are willing to confront their people on the level of social and political evils (a confrontation long overdue), but there is less and less confrontation on matters of doctrine and personal morality. If and when it comes to the stage that priests hesitate to preach that private moral offenses (such as impurity) are sinful or that some novel ideas are doctrinally dangerous, then we shall have shifted radically from the Pauline idea of the service that an apostle must render to those for whom he is responsible. (Need I remark that in the past we have often been too free in labeling actions as sinful and in damning legitimate theological differences, but here I am talking about the *principle* of correction and confrontation.) Paul himself wrestled with the objection that in such correction one may lose the love of those corrected, but at least from his own side he saw the correction itself as an act of love ("If I love you the more, am I to be loved the less?" —II Cor 12:15).

Often for a priest a particularly anguishing moment in this problem of correction comes in turning away someone from the sacraments or "from the Church," generally in loyalty to the demands of canon law. This action is quite foreign to the modern understanding of care for others. Once again we all recognize that the resort to excommunication has been too frequent in the past and that any community preoccupied with excluding people is more a sect than a church. But granted the danger of abuse, we cannot escape the basic point at issue: Is the Christian message a two-edged sword that at times divides and turns away? If one voices the objection that exclusion belongs to God alone, he must face the fact that from its earliest days and with the approval of its most notable spokesmen the Church has exercised the power of exclusion, especially in doctrinal and moral matters. And so a protest against all excommunication is not simply a protest against canon law but against the preachers

of the Gospel. No matter what shade of interpretation one gives
to Matt 18:15-18,[19] the passage is clear evidence of the antiquity of ecclesiastical procedure for a type of authoritative
action against members of the community. Paul, the champion
of Christian freedom, is extremely authoritarian when it comes
to this matter: "If anyone refuses to obey what we say in this
letter, note that man and have nothing to do with him, that he
may be ashamed" (II Thess 3:14; see also I Cor 5:1-5). If this
is not the side of Paul's character that we spontaneously remember, it is because he knew how to temper severity with love
—and that is not the least part of the lesson about correction
that he teaches us (II Cor 2:7).

There are undoubtedly other services that could be mentioned in discussing the role of the apostle and how it has influenced the ideal of priestly service to others. As stated at the
beginning, I have taken for granted the more obvious aspects of
apostolic service, namely, the manifestations of a generous and
tireless outpouring of oneself for men in the imitation of Jesus
Christ; and I have concentrated on forms of service that might
otherwise be neglected. At the end, lest the picture that has
emerged be out of focus, let me emphasize that precisely what I
have taken for granted is the core without which the other forms
of apostolic service, albeit necessary, would not have much
meaning. The Paul whom we have made our paradigm of
apostolic service for men has summed it up better than anyone
else: "I will most gladly spend and be spent for you" (II Cor
12:15).

3. The Presbyter-Bishop

We have said that the image of the apostle has shaped the

---

[19] It is uncertain whether the Matthean formula refers to the
imposition or removal of an obligation through an authoritative
doctrinal decision (a power that would affect people indirectly
through their actions) or the power to impose or remove a ban of
excommunication (a power that would affect people directly). The
latter interpretation seems more likely for Matt 18:15-18, while
the former is possible for Matt 16:19.

ideal of priestly service. However, in at least one important aspect the role of the Pauline apostle was quite different from the role of the later priest. The apostle was a missionary figure, founding communities, but then moving on and maintaining contact with his communities through letters, emissaries, and occasional visits. The priest, when he emerges in Christian history, is predominantly a residential figure, living among the congregation for whom he cares. The NT paradigm for this type of residential care is the presbyter-bishop. In Chapter Two we shall discuss in detail the origin of bishops in the NT churches; but for the moment let us follow the common scholarly opinion that, where they existed in the post-Pauline churches, presbyters and bishops were for all practical purposes the same, that as a group[20] they were responsible for the pastoral care of those churches, and that we have in the Pastoral Epistles, I Peter, and Acts a picture of their activities in the 80's, if not earlier.

From such NT works it would seem that the presbyter-bishops took up where the Pauline apostles left off, being responsible for the continued care of churches founded by the apostles (whether the presbyter-bishops were appointed directly by the apostles or came on the scene only sometime later). In the Pastorals we find delegates[21] of Paul (or at least his disciples, if the Pastorals were written after Paul's death) spelling out what is expected of the presbyter-bishops as to character and to work. The character traits are highly institutional: the presbyter-bishops must be above reproach, temperate, sensible, dignified, hospitable, apt teachers, gentle and not quarrelsome (I Tim 3:1-7; Titus 1:7-9). As one reads this list of staid virtues, one may wonder whether Paul would have made a good presbyter-bishop; for at times he was certainly not temperate (Gal 3:1),

---

[20] We do not seem to have in the NT (with the possible exception of III John) the situation found in the letters of Ignatius of Antioch, where there is a single bishop with the presbyters as his helpers.

[21] The idea that Timothy was the bishop of Ephesus and Titus was the bishop of Crete has no explicit basis in the Pastoral Epistles. Rather these men are pictured as delegates of the apostle checking on the authorities of the local churches.

nor dignified (Gal 5:12), nor gentle (Philip 3:2). But this observation is not surprising—the apostle is a charismatic and not an institutionalized figure: his are the new frontiers and the adventurism of spiritual conquest. A more pedestrian pattern is held up for the presbyter-bishop (although in NT thought he too would have a charism—I Cor 12:28 speaks of "the charism of administration"!); he is to be the one who can manage a household well (I Tim 3:4-5); his is the task of organizing, stabilizing, and preventing dangerous innovation (Titus 1:9). Undoubtedly, in the mood of our anti-institutional times, the apostle will be seen as the more exciting and sympathetic figure when compared with the presbyter-bishop. Yet in the long run without the permanent institutional element the work of the apostle would soon have vanished.

Some aspects of the NT portrait of the presbyter-bishop are of great interest as formative elements for the later priesthood. We note, for instance, that the presbyter-bishop must meet certain requirements beyond those of virtuous character: he is not to be a recent convert, nor married twice (I Tim 3:2, 6). Here we have an example of the Church setting its own stipulations for its special ministry. Such qualifications would be unintelligible in a purely charismatic office, but they are quite understandable in a partially charismatic institution established along prudential lines. An individual recent convert might make an excellent presbyter-bishop, but in an institutional mentality one has to sacrifice the occasional individual on the basis of the general percentage whereby a recent convert often needs time to mature. We can find a similar approach in the priesthood today where dioceses are setting automatic retirement ages, even though we all know that some individuals are perfectly capable of competent service long after the retirement age—the individuals are sacrificed to the general welfare. Curiously, at the same time when the priesthood is being put on a more professional institutional basis than ever before (retirement plans; salaries rather than stipends), we find existing regulations attacked, not on the grounds that they are unwise, but on the grounds of doubt whether the Church has the right to make such regulations. I am thinking particularly of the law of clerical celibacy when it is attacked with the contention that the Church cannot institutionalize a charism. As I have said, I am not going to enter the debate of whether this is *wise* legislation; but I would certainly defend the Church's right to make such a regulation for its own ministry, precisely because the priesthood is heir to an institutional antecedent (presbyter-bishop) as well as to more charismatic antecedents (disciple and apostle). Celibacy is not unrelated to discipleship (it is for the sake of the kingdom of heaven that the challenge to celibacy is issued —Matt 19:12); nor is it unrelated to apostleship (Paul wishes that the other missionary apostles were unmarried as he is— I Cor 9:5 with 7:7-8). We find already in the Pastoral Epistles the tendency to introduce regulations about the married status of presbyter-bishops. The regulation of I Tim 3:2 that a widower who has remarried cannot be a presbyter-bishop is not really different *in kind* from the later church law that a married man cannot serve as a priest.

The portrait of the presbyter-bishop in the Pastorals complements indirectly some of what we have said about the types of service rendered by an apostle. The presbyter-bishop, for instance, has the duty of correcting and censoring: "He must hold firm to the sure word he was taught so that he may be able to give instructions in sound doctrine and to confute objectors. For there are many who are out of control . . . who must be silenced" (Titus 1:9-11; see also Acts 20:30). Yet, if we may apply II Tim 2:24 to him, he must be kindly and forebearing in his teaching. The presbyter-bishop (probably) has the duty of caring for the community finances; this is implied in the stress that he has to be able to manage a household and should not be greedy about money (I Tim 3:3-4; also I Peter 5:2).[22]

---

[22] In Hellenistic writing *episkopos* ("bishop") was the title of an official responsible for the financial affairs of a cultic organization. We shall point out in Chapter Two that there are officials in the Qumran (Dead Sea Scroll) community who are remarkably similar to bishops—these men managed the community property. H. Küng, *The Church*, p. 400, dismisses too easily the managerial or economic role of the bishop (partly because Küng does not appreciate the importance of the Qumran parallelism). He says that, if bishops had an economic function, the individual Christians at Corinth

Often today there is a criticism of bishops and pastors, not only
in terms of their being overly involved in administration (a criticism that may be justified), but on the grounds that priesthood
should have nothing to do with administration. This criticism is
sometimes supported by an appeal to the examples of Jesus, of
his disciples, and of Paul, none of whom were administrators.
Such an argument neglects the presbyter-bishop as an antecedent
of the priest. Yet, if the NT does show the presbyter-bishop as
an administrator, it is also careful to give him a pastoral image,
surrounding him with shepherd symbolism. In Acts 20:28-29
Paul tells the presbyters of Ephesus, "Care for the flock in which
the Holy Spirit has made you bishops to feed the church of the
Lord which he obtained with his own blood. I know that after
my departure fierce wolves will come in among you, not sparing
the flock." In I Peter 5:2-4 the writer exhorts his fellow elders
or presbyters: "Tend the flock of God that is in your charge,
exercising your episcopate willingly . . . being examples to the
flock, so that when the Chief Shepherd appears, you will obtain
the unfading crown of glory." The role of shepherd seems to be
coupled with that of teacher in Eph 4:11.

The image of the presbyter-bishop also contributed to the
development of an authority structure in the later priesthood.
We see this if we go beyond the NT to the time of Ignatius of
Antioch (*ca.* 110) when in many communities one bishop had
emerged as the head of a college of presbyters.[23] Ignatius' direc-
tives pertinent to the authority of the bishop would make the
most authoritarian bishop of our times blush—for Ignatius
episcopacy, like cleanliness, was next to godliness! "You have
only to acknowledge God and the bishop, and all is well; for a
man who honors his bishop is himself honored by God" (*Smyr-*

would not have had to put aside money to contribute to the collection for Jerusalem. But we do not know that there were bishops at
Corinth!

[23] We say in "many communities" because we have no proof that
the church structure described by Ignatius was universal. Moreover,
even within the Ignatian corpus there is no mention of a bishop in
the letter to the Romans. It is interesting that in mid-2nd century,
if that is when the *Shepherd of Hermas* was written, the Roman
church seems still to be ruled by a presbyterate (Vision II ɪᴠ 3).

naeans 9:1). "Let us be careful not to oppose the bishop, so that we may be subject to God" (*Ephesians* 5:3). "When you are obedient to your bishop as though he were Jesus Christ, it is clear to me that you are living after the manner of Jesus Christ himself" (*Trallians* 2:1). "I must count you blessed who are united with your bishop, just as the Church is united with Jesus Christ, and Jesus Christ is united with the Father" (*Ephesians* 5:1). "It comes to this: that we ought not just have the name of Christians but be Christians in reality, not like some people who acknowledge a man as bishop verbally but take no notice of him in their actions" (*Magnesians* 4:1). "As the Lord was united to the Father and never acted independently of Him ... so you yourselves must never act independently of your bishop and presbyters" (*Magnesians* 7:1). "Make sure that no step affecting the Church is ever taken without the bishop" (*Smyrnaeans* 8:1).

Obviously such respect for the bishop can serve as a powerful weapon against disunity and budding heresy, and this is why Ignatius emphasized it—the presence of the bishop was as sure a sign for the local church as was the presence of Jesus Christ for the whole Church (*Smyrnaeans* 8:2). Yet we must realize that Ignatius was speaking to small local churches; we may compare the Ignatian bishop and presbyters to a pastor and curates in a one-parish town. Authority exercised in such a small area had a good chance of being humanized by intimacy and friendship. Within the institutional framework of the later Church when the bishop ruled a greater area and social customs rendered him more remote from his people, the type of emphasis that Ignatius put on episcopal authority would easily lead to a hierarchical absolutism. As a corrective to this development we recall that the various antecedents of the historical priesthood are capable of modifying each other. Precisely because the priesthood is heir to the role of the presbyter-bishop, there is a place in the priesthood for a hierarchy of authority, but because the priesthood is heir to the role of the disciple of Jesus all authority must be modified by the ideal that one disciple is not to lord it over another or seek the first place in the manner of worldly institutions. This modification of authority was recog-

nized already in NT times in the very history of the presby-
terate-episcopate, for the author of I Pet 5:1-3 insisted that the
presbyters had the duty of overseeing (i.e., being bishops over)
the flock, but he warned them that this gave them no right to
be domineering.

4. The One Who Presided at the Eucharist

We saw at the beginning of the discussion of the NT evidence that the Christian priesthood, replacing the priesthood of
Israel, emerged only when the Eucharist came to be understood
as an unbloody sacrifice replacing the bloody sacrifices of the
Temple. Yet in the discussion of the actual NT antecedents of
the Christian priesthood I have kept till last the role of the one
who presided at the Eucharist, the role that caused the Christian
ministry to be understood precisely as a priesthood. In part my
reason for so doing was to dramatize what a rich concept of
ministry we could have even independently of the sacramental
—a corrective of an older tendency to think of the ministry as
almost exclusively a sacramental role ("a man can be a splendid
priest if he does nothing else but offer Mass"). It is significant
that the NT does not attribute much eucharistic functioning to
any of the three roles we have already discussed. In the descrip-
tions of the presbyter-bishop nothing is said of his presiding at
the Eucharist (although the bishop did preside in the time of
Ignatius and the NT silence may be by accident). Paul never
mentions that he presided at the Eucharist,[24] although Acts
20:11 may be interpreted to cast him in that role (if Acts is
not retrojecting a later church picture). Some activity in relation
to the Eucharist is implied for the Twelve disciples, for it is
recorded that the words "Do this in commemoration of me"

---

[24] The fact that Paul mentions the Eucharist in only one of his
letters (I Cor 10:16-17; 11:23-34) weakens the force of the silence
in his case. Yet it is worth noting that in the eighteen months that
he was in Corinth (Acts 18:11), he seems to have baptized only
two people and a household (I Cor 1:14-15). Evidently he was not
primarily involved in administering sacraments.

were addressed to them at the Last Supper (Luke 22:19—the addressees are not specified in I Cor 11:24). In point of fact, however, in the NT we are never told that any of them actually presided at the Eucharist.

The very silence of the NT about who did preside is my other reason for keeping this discussion of the sacramental antecedents of the Christian priesthood till last. The eucharistic words of Jesus are reported in the NT in two very ancient independent liturgical formulas (Mark/Matthew and Luke/Paul); there is frequent mention, especially in Acts, of the breaking of the bread; but we are never clearly told who presided by breaking the bread or saying the words.[25] Thus there is simply no compelling evidence for the classic thesis that the members of the Twelve always presided when they were present, and that there was a chain of ordination passing the power of presiding at the Eucharist from the Twelve to missionary apostles to presbyter-bishops. (Although we do not intend to discuss the origin of other priestly powers that were subsequently designated as sacramental, the same lack of evidence would call into question the chain theory of the communication of the power to forgive sins, anoint the sick, etc.) The only thing of which we can be reasonably sure is that someone must have presided at the eucharistic meals and that those who participated acknowledged his right to preside. How one got the right to preside and whether it endured beyond a single instance we do not know; but a more plausible substitute for the chain theory is the thesis that sacramental "powers" were part of the mission of the Church and that there were diverse ways in which the Church (or the communities) designated individuals to exercise those powers—the essential element always being church or com-

---

[25] Some have suggested that the prophets *regularly* presided at the Eucharist (Acts 13:1-2 has prophets "liturgizing," and *Didache* 10:7 would permit prophets to give thanks [*eucharistein*]; the "ministry [*leitourgia*] of prophets" in *Didache* 15:1 is related to celebrating the Eucharist on the Lord's Day in 14:1). H. Lietzmann has advanced the thesis that there were eucharistic meals in which the institutional words of Jesus were not recited, but his position depends heavily on an inference from the much later liturgy of Serapion.

munity consent (which was tantamount to ordination, whether
or not that consent was signified by a special ceremony such as
the laying on of hands).

As the Church grew larger such consent had to be regular-
ized, not only as to ordination ceremony but also as to the type
of individuals who could preside at the Eucharist, so that presiding eventually became the exclusive privilege of bishops and
presbyters. The *Didache* may have been written just at the
turning point; for, while the wandering prophets are not for-
bidden to hold Eucharist (10:7), there is an instruction (15:1),
in connection with other instructions on celebrating the Eucharist (14), to appoint bishops and deacons who will render for
the community the ministry *(leitourgia)* of the prophets. In the
year 96 *I Clement* 44:4 speaks of the sin of ejecting from office
"men who have offered the sacrificial gifts of the episcopate
worthily"—perhaps a reference to bishops celebrating the
Eucharist. In the churches addressed by Ignatius of Antioch
about fifteen years later it is well established that only the
bishop or one of the presbyters whom he designates can preside
over the Eucharist (*Smyrnaeans* 8:1). In other words about the
turn of the century (or a little earlier) two roles that once may
have been separate had been joined: the role of the presbyter-
bishop and the role of the celebrant of the Eucharist. Now, besides caring for the doctrinal, moral, and even temporal needs
of his flock, the bishop (together with his presbyters) is to care
for the community sacramentally as well. The communities
addressed by Ignatius are told to obey the bishop and the pres-
bytery, *breaking one bread with them,* for that is the medicine of
immortality (*Ephesians* 20:2).

At the same period when, in some churches at least, the
bishop or designated presbyters had become the sole celebrants
of the Eucharist, these men were also being considered the successors of the apostles—not only in the sense that they were the
resident authorities in communities founded by apostles, but also
in the sense that they were to the later church what the apostles
were to the primitive church. In Chapter Two we shall discuss
this problem in detail; but for our present purposes it is sufficient to note that when sub-apostolic writings, like *I Clement*

and the Ignatian letters, speak of "apostles," often they have blended together the role of the Twelve disciples and the role of the Pauline missionary apostle. *I Clement* 42—44 pictures the "apostles" appointing bishops who were in turn commissioned to appoint successors, so that one basic ministry is transmitted in lineal descent. (As we shall see there is some evidence that Paul may have appointed presbyter-bishops, but no evidence that the Twelve did—thus Clement's testimony may be somewhat confused.) Ignatius, *Smyrnaeans,* 8:1, tells the people: "Follow your bishop, every one of you, as obediently as Jesus Christ followed the Father; and *follow your presbyters as you would follow the apostles."* Thus, the other two roles we have discussed, that of the (Twelve) disciples and that of the missionary apostles, are beginning to be blended with the role of the presbyter-bishop, now the celebrant of the Eucharist. That such a combination of roles would not be contrary to the spirit of the NT is seen, for instance, in Acts 1:20 which refers to the office or position of the Twelve as an *episkopē*. Peter, the most prominent member of the Twelve, is shown referring to himself as a presbyter (not necessarily in the technical sense of presbyter-bishop) in I Peter 5:1, while John 21:15-17 attributes to Peter the task of shepherding—a favorite symbolism for the presbyter-bishop. By the end of the 2nd century, if not earlier, the blending of diverse NT roles has been carried through in its essentials, and the full-blown concept of the Christian priest emerges as the result.[26] In the course of time other modifying factors would enter in, as dioceses grew bigger and began to contain many parishes, and as the clerical hierarchy was affected by civil models, particularly in the age of feudalism. But these developments, however important, go beyond the area of the present discussion which aims at clarifying the biblical background of the priesthood.

---

[26] Subsequently, for a long time, most of the reflections about priesthood will be centered on *the bishop,* to whom the presbyters are a collegiate board of advisors and helpers. Until size and spread to rural areas created a new situation, all that we would consider the normal pastoral and sacramental duties of a priest were exercised regularly by the bishop himself.

*   *   *

By way of concluding this chapter, I would maintain that the diversified background treated above constitutes both the grandeur and the weakness of the priesthood. Yes, the *grandeur,* because the priesthood has adopted and adapted to itself some of the most prominent NT roles and, consequently, enfolded a tremendous idealistic wealth—the spiritual ideals of the disciples of Jesus, the spirit of dedicated service embodied in Paul, the tried and true virtues of the presbyter-bishop, the dignity of sacramental ministry associated with the bread of life and the cup of the new covenant. In short, the priesthood aspires to what was regarded as a model of Christian behavior by various stages of NT thought.

But this aspiration is also a *weakness* because it asks of one man, the priest, more than was asked of any man who played one of the NT roles we have discussed. In fact, as we have suggested, the combination of ideals and functions cloaks the tension that existed between the different character traits demanded by the various NT roles. I believe that some of today's "identity crisis" among priests reflects the diversified background of the priesthood. One priest will persuasively argue that his task is to administer the sacraments and be a good pastor to his parishioners; another will contend that the Christian ministry must be apostolic and reach out to the missions of our day, for instance, to the inner-city areas where urbanization has degraded the image of God that is man's glory; and still another priest will maintain that above all a priest is to be a spiritual man, with eyes fixed on his heavenly master. As the respective proponents rightly claim, each of these views of the priesthood has backing in the NT—unfortunately, however, the proponents often do not recognize that there is basis in the NT for another view as well, and so they judge that the advocates of the other view(s) are not good priests.

I hope that this study may help in a modest way to clarify the legitimacy of pluralism in priestly work and temperament. Yet I do not want to leave the impression that there is no common denominator in all the NT roles I have described and that, consequently, diverse modern views of a priest's task should not come under the one rubric of priesthood. At the risk of emphasizing the obvious, I would point out one very important common element in the four NT roles described in this chapter and an element that I think should remain prominent in every diverse form of priestly ministry today, namely, closeness to Jesus Christ. The whole nature of discipleship is a patterning on the master, and what is expected of the *disciple* flows from the all-demanding call to follow Jesus. The primary definition of the Pauline *apostle* is in terms of his being a servant of Jesus Christ. The pastoral model held up for the *presbyter-bishop* is that of shepherd,. a symbol used of Jesus as well (John 10:11, 14; Matt 25:31-32; Heb 13:20; I Peter 2:25). And, of course, the *one who presides at the Eucharist* has the task of proclaiming the death of the Lord until he comes again (I Cor 11:26). In other words, all NT forms of what would eventually come together under the heading of priestly activity have the task of bearing witness to Jesus. An older piety tried to give expression to this when it spoke of the priest as "another Christ." I mentioned that some of the "identity crisis" among priests today may be related to different conceptions of priestly activity; but on a deeper level I would think that the only identity crisis truly worthy of the name occurs when, amidst the legitimate differences in priestly work, the priest begins to forget that it is Jesus Christ to whom he is bearing witness. Whatever other claim he may make about what he does, in order to know who he is, a priest must be able to join with Paul in issuing the challenge, "Become imitators of me as I am of Christ" (I Cor 11:1).

CHAPTER 2
ARE THE BISHOPS
THE SUCCESSORS
OF THE APOSTLES?

Since in many ways the bishop is the chief priest of an area, in describing the biblical background of the Catholic priesthood I have described the basic development of the episcopate as well. (As pointed out in note 26 above, once the term "priest" was introduced to describe those in the special ministry, for a long time its principal use was in reference to the bishop, not to presbyters.) However, there is one crucial aspect of the development of the episcopate that I have but touched upon, namely, its relation to apostleship. We shall now concentrate on this question, for it is as successors to the apostles that bishops have exercised their great influence in the history of Roman Catholicism.

I. The New Testament Evidence about
Apostles and Bishops

The necessity for a deeper Catholic probing of the NT evidence concerning the relation of bishops to apostles was brought home to me by the remark of a distinguished Protestant scholar who was commenting on the documents of Vatican II.

He asked me where were the exegetes when *Lumen Gentium* 18
and the *Decree on the Bishops' Pastoral Office* 2 repeated without significant qualification the age-old dictum that the bishops
were the successors of the apostles. Of course, he did not mean
that Vatican II should have contradicted that dictum; but since
modern biblical subtleties were reflected in many conciliar statements, he wondered why there seemed to be no awareness of
biblical difficulties when it came to this affirmation. No NT
exegete can read it without asking the obvious question that is
not broached in the documents of Vatican II: Which apostles?[27]
The NT contains several very different views about what an
apostle was; and it is important, nay even decisive, to know to
which form of apostolic activity the bishops are to be considered
successors. I plan below to discuss only two NT views of the
apostolate;[28] but since these two are the most prominent, even
such a limited discussion will bring out the complexities of the
problem and the necessity of a more nuanced understanding of
apostolic succession.

A. Bishops and the Lucan Picture of the Twelve Apostles

In the view of the author of Acts the chief apostles of the
primitive Church were the Twelve disciples who had been with
Jesus during his lifetime. This view may be called Lucan if we
understand that, while Luke is its chief spokesman, he is far
from its only proponent. The various Gospels make a connection between the Twelve disciples and the apostolate by having
the disciples *sent out (apostellein*—Mark 6:7) during the min-

---

[27] There was a discussion at Vatican II as to whether the bishops
succeeded to "the college of the apostles" or to individual apostles,
but the question that exegetes would pose is much more fundamental.

[28] For a fuller treatment of the problem with ample bibliography
see R. Schnackenburg, "Apostolicity: The Present Position of Stud-
ies," *One in Christ* 6 (1970), pp. 243-73.

istry[29] and by having an apostolic charge directed to them by the risen Jesus (see p. 27 above). Mark 6:30 and Matt 10:2 speak of the disciples as apostles; in fact, Matthew speaks of "the Twelve apostles," as does Rev 21:14.

How valid is this view? The fact that it appears more frequently in the late NT writings suggests to some scholars that it is a fictional touch designed to magnify the memory of the Twelve disciples of Jesus, who actually were important during his ministry but, except for Peter and John, not particularly important in the Church. However, the majority of scholars still find persuasive the evidence that the Twelve disciples of Jesus were considered apostles of the Church from the beginning. For instance, in a formulation dating from the first years of Christianity (I Cor 15:5), Paul passes on the tradition that the risen Jesus was seen by the Twelve—a vision that was an essential constituent of the apostolate. The fact that each of the Synoptic Gospels preserves a list of the names of the Twelve indicates that the idea of the Twelve remained an important memory for the Church. (The lists are scarcely a recent creation in the Gospels, for the names of the lesser members of the Twelve are confused, probably because they are being forgotten, even though the concept of the Twelve as a whole is not forgotten.) But if we accept the historicity of the Twelve as apostles, the thesis that there were *only* Twelve apostles is certainly a later simplification. There were many apostles in the early days, but the Twelve had a special place in the apostolate, not so much because of their missionary activities (we shall see that there is no evidence that most of them left the Jersualem area) but because they had been the intimate companions of Jesus.

Turning now to a more specific consideration of the Lucan view of the Twelve apostles, we find several areas of scholarly debate. *First,* many argue that Luke confines apostleship exclusively to the Twelve, and some even suggest that Luke goes out of his way to show that Paul was not an apostle. I am not sure that the Lucan picture of apostleship is so simple. If the

---

[29] See note 18 above. It would have been the understanding of the evangelists that in sending out the Twelve Jesus was signifying his intention that they participate in his present and future ministry.

other Gospels show a sending out of the Twelve during the ministry in order to connect apostolate and discipleship, Luke 10:1 has an additional sending out *(apostellein)* of seventy or seventy-two disciples—in other words, in his account of Jesus' ministry Luke may be foreshadowing a wider group of apostles. Of course, for Luke the Twelve were uniquely close to Jesus, and so they have a privileged apostolate not possessed by others, even by Paul.[30] Also, in the post-resurrectional period Luke would stress a difference between the Twelve and Paul: the risen Jesus appears to the Twelve before his ascension, but to Paul after the ascension; and so there is a different quality in the respective appearances. Yet Luke does not refuse the title of "apostle" to Paul (and Barnabas—Acts 14:4, 14).[31] Indeed, in the latter part of Acts Luke pays Paul the compliment of attributing to him the same type of sermons and miracles that are attributed to Peter (who is the first of the apostles) in the early part of Acts. Thus, I would maintain that for Luke the apostleship of the Twelve is more a question of *par excellence* than of absolute exclusivity.

A *second* debated area in reference to Acts is the accuracy of Luke's description of the activities of the Twelve in the primitive Church. It is quite clear that Luke has simplified the picture in order to highlight the power of the Twelve at Jerusalem, but

---

[30] Scholars often call attention to the fact that the two candidates who are put forward for admission to the Twelve in place of Judas have to meet the condition of having been with Jesus during his ministry (Acts 1:21-23). I do not think it correct, however, to conclude that this was a Lucan condition for being considered an apostle—all that can be proved from the text is that this was a condition for having part in *the apostolate of the Twelve*. One must resort to other passages to see if Luke identifies all apostleship with the apostleship of the Twelve.

[31] The suggestion that here Acts draws upon a pre-Lucan source wherein there was no difficulty about the apostleship of Paul and Barnabas does not change the fact that Luke did not edit out this use of "apostles." Unless we are gratuitously to assume carelessness on Luke's part, the obvious inference is that Luke did not exclude the apostleship of Paul and Barnabas. The objection that "apostles" is missing in vs. 14 in Codex Bezae and some Old Latin and Syriac versional witnesses is not particularly impressive.

at the core of his idealization there is probably a greater historical substratum than recent German commentaries on Acts have been willing to allow. Here I cannot debate the historicity of each point in the Lucan description; but I will concentrate on a general picture that I judge plausible. On the other side of the coin, the reader should be aware that the Lucan description may actually be more defective by way of silence than by way of exaggeration. Luke tells us relatively little about the Twelve, and they may have been much more active than the NT shows us.

1. What the Lucan Apostles Were Not

Let us begin by weeding out some misconceptions or confusions about the portrait of the Twelve in Acts. Luke does not show these apostles as missionaries. Although in Luke 24:47 there is a prediction about preaching to all nations, and although at the beginning of Acts (1:8) Jesus says to the Twelve apostles whom he has chosen (1:2, 13), "You shall be my witnesses in Jerusalem and in all Judea and Samaria, and to the ends of the earth," in fact, there is little evidence in Acts that the Twelve were active outside Jerusalem. It was the Hellenists and not the Twelve who spread Christianity to Samaria, for Peter and John were sent to Samaria to extend Jerusalem's approval of a venture that was already well under way (Acts 8:1-15). And as for "the ends of the earth," although Peter hesitantly accepted into the Christian fold a God-fearer (a Gentile inclined toward Judaism—Cornelius in Acts 10), the great missionaries to the Gentiles were Paul and Barnabas, not the members of the Twelve. (Once again the Twelve were called upon to give approval to these innovations regarding Gentiles—Acts 11:1-18; 15:1-12). Thus, in the Lucan view the Twelve as a group were not personally involved in missionary activities, although they had a certain power of approving them. Our other historical information, although very sparse, seems to confirm the Lucan picture in which the role of the Twelve was not primarily missionary. Several passages in Matthew where Jesus addresses the disciples would be very hard to understand if there was an early tradition that the Twelve had gone on the Gentile mission: "Go nowhere among the Gentiles . . . but rather go to the lost sheep of the house of Israel"; "You will not have gone through all the towns of Israel before the Son of Man comes" (Matt 10:5-6, 23 —note that these passages are from the Mission Sermon where the apostolate of the Twelve is retrojected into the ministry of Jesus). We can give no real credence to later traditions that the Twelve scattered to various corners of the world;[32] in part these traditions arose from regional pride, as it became fashionable for each church to defend its antiquity and apostolic origin. For only two of the Twelve is there any proof of a wider ranging ministry: the evidence that Peter went to Rome is good, and the evidence that John son of Zebedee went to Asia Minor and Ephesus is worthy of consideration.

If the Twelve as a group were not primarily missionaries, neither were they bishops. There is no evidence in Acts that any one of the Twelve presided over a local church. It is generally agreed that James, who was the leader of the Jerusalem church (although not called a bishop), was the brother of the Lord and not the same as the James of Alphaeus mentioned in the lists of the Twelve.[33] Although Peter has sometimes been called the bishop of Antioch, there is no evidence in Acts (see 11:19-20) that he either brought Christianity there or presided over the community. (The weakness of the tradition of "the Chair of St. Peter at Antioch" was implicitly recognized when the feast [February 22] was removed from the calendar several years

---

[32] These traditions make their appearance in the apocryphal writings of the 2nd and 3rd centuries: the apostles were primarily concerned with the Gentiles; or, for twelve years they addressed the Jews, and then they turned to the Gentiles; or, the earth was partitioned among the Twelve for missionary activity. (See W. Bauer, "The Picture of the Apostle in Early Christian Tradition," in E. Hennecke and W. Schneemelcher, *New Testament Apocrypha* [Philadelphia: Westminster, 1965], II, pp. 43-44.) Eusebius, *History*, III, 1, reports: "The holy apostles and disciples of our Savior were scattered over the whole world. Tradition tells us that Thomas was chosen for Parthia, Andrew for Scythia. . . ."

[33] Acts 1:13-14 makes a clear distinction between the Twelve and the brothers of the Lord.

ago.) A more ancient tradition reports that Peter was the first bishop of Rome.[34] This seems quite unlikely from what we know of Christianity at Rome. From archaeology (Christian burials) and from Roman history (Suetonius' reference to Claudius' expulsion of the Jews from Rome *ca.* 49, *"impulsore Chresto,"* i.e., caused by their arguments about Christ) it is plausible that Christianity reached Rome in the early 40's, while Peter was still in Jerusalem. The supposition that, when he did come to Rome (presumably in the 60's), he took over and became the first bishop represents a retrojection of later church order. As we pointed out in note 23, our evidence would suggest that the emergence of a single bishop, distinct from the college of presbyter-bishops, came relatively late in the Roman church, perhaps not until well into the 2nd century. Leaders, such as Linus, Cletus, and Clement, known to us from the early Roman church, were probably prominent presbyter-bishops but not necessarily "monarchical" bishops. The latest detailed work on the subject[35] maintains:

> That Peter founded the Church at Rome is extremely doubtful and that he served as its first bishop (as we understand the term today) for even one year, much less the twenty-five-year period that is claimed for him, is an unfounded tradition that can be traced back to a point no earlier than the third century. The liturgical celebrations which relate to the ascent of Peter to the Roman episcopacy do not begin to make their appearance until the fourth century at the earliest. Furthermore, there is no mention of the Roman episcopacy of Peter in the New Testament, I

---

[34] The tradition is clear in "The Letter of Clement to James" in the Pseudo-Clementine Literature (origins, perhaps, in the early 3rd century). But one can argue that the list of Roman bishops mentioned by Hegesippus in mid-2nd century (a list no longer extant but recoverable from Epiphanius) mentioned Peter and Paul as first joint bishops of Rome. There is little in the NT to support the thesis that Peter was a bishop, except for the fact that I Peter 5:1 has Peter speak as a presbyter—but does this mean presbyter-bishop or simply "elder"? The latter is possible even though the other presbyters whom Peter addresses have episcopal functions. See note 44 below.

[35] D. W. O'Connor, *Peter in Rome* (New York: Columbia University, 1969), p. 207.

Clement, or the epistles of Ignatius. The tradition is only
dimly discerned in Hegesippus and may be implied in the
suspect letter of Dionysius of Corinth to the Romans [ca.
170]. By the third century, however, the early assumptions
based upon invention or vague, unfounded tradition have
been transformed into "facts" of history.

Lest I cause unnecessary scandal, may I point out that, in my
judgment, the probability that Peter was not the first "monarchical" bishop of Rome does not weaken in any way the claim
that the position of primacy held by Peter has been continued
in the Church and is now enjoyed by the bishop of Rome. The
two roles of primate and of bishop of Rome, separate at the
beginning, were subsequently joined. (Even the most conservative Catholic would have to admit this, since Peter was primate
among the Twelve long before he went to Rome.)
　　The fact that the Twelve apostles were not bishops or local
church leaders and, in fact, coexisted in Jerusalem with James
who was the local church leader, is one reason why exegetes
have a difficulty about the bishops being successors to these
apostles. The apostolate of the Twelve and the presbyterate-
episcopate (or at least local church leadership) were different
roles that seemingly existed simultaneously. Some have thought
of succession in terms of powers being transmitted, especially
sacramental powers. It has been customary to argue from the
command to commemorate Jesus in the Eucharist (Luke
22:19), from the command to baptize (Matt 28:19), and from
the statement about the forgiveness of sins (John 20:23)—all
addressed to an audience that consisted of or included the
Twelve—that the apostles exercised these powers in the Church
and then passed them on to the ones whom they ordained. But,
with the exception of Baptism, we have virtually no evidence
of the exercise of these powers by the Twelve (for the Eucharist
see pp. 40-41 above), even though that exercise is quite plausible. One may persuasively argue that the sacramental "powers"
were given *to the Christian community* in the persons of the
Twelve; and while the Twelve themselves may have baptized,
presided at the Eucharist and forgiven sins, the Church may
also have recognized the sacramental authority of others who

were not ordained by the Twelve. In other words, if the sacramental power resides in the Church, it can be given to those whom the Church designates or acknowledges, without a lineal connection to the Twelve. It is interesting that the Church recognizes the privilege of any Christian (or even non-Christian) to baptize, even though in Matthew the command to baptize was addressed to the Eleven.

Moreover, the theory about passing on powers through ordination faces the serious obstacle that the NT does not show the Twelve laying hands on bishops either as successors or as auxiliaries in administering sacraments. A possible partial exception is the laying of hands on the Hellenist leaders in Acts 6:6, but even there it is not clear who lays hands, the Twelve or the community as a whole. And if we confine ourselves to the idea of succession, we may assert that according to NT thought there can be no successors to the Twelve as such. (This is not so radical an idea as may first seem, for Christian theology has traditionally taught that certain aspects of apostleship were not transferable.) The symbolism of the Twelve is associated with the idea ᵗhat the Christian movement represents the renewal of Israel. Thus, just as at its founding Israel consisted of twelve tribes descended from the twelve sons of Jacob-Israel, so at the moment when Jesus renews Israel there are his Twelve disciples to proclaim the good news of what has happened. By this symbolism the Twelve are unique. When Judas betrays Jesus and reduces the number to eleven, someone has to be elected to fill out the Twelve. But when the individual members die, they are not replaced; rather, as the founders of the renewed Israel, they are immortalized. According to Rev 21:14, the twelve foundations of the city that is the heavenly Jerusalem have on them "the twelve names of the Twelve apostles of the Lamb." Furthermore, they cannot be replaced because, precisely as the Twelve, they have an eschatological role to play: in the judgment scene they have been appointed to sit on (twelve) thrones judging the twelve tribes of Israel (Luke 22:30; Matt 19:28).

2. *The Role of the Twelve according to Luke*

We have said that the Twelve, in the Lucan picture, were

not primarily missionaries, nor local church leaders, nor men
who ordained others and passed on powers to them. (Perhaps
it may be wise to emphasize here again the awkwardness of the
argument from silence; the Twelve may have done more than
Luke records.) Because of these limitations we have seen how
difficult it is to claim that the NT bishops were in succession to
the Twelve. However, if we lay aside the eschatological symbolism of the Twelve, they played a very definite role in the primitive Church described in Acts. Let us discuss that role now.

In Acts the Twelve figure prominently in two major decisions affecting the growth and future of the Church. We shall
first describe the decisions and then analyze the role of the
Twelve. The first is narrated in Acts 6:1-6. Scholars agree that
the question of the Hellenists was a much more serious problem
than is evident *prima facie*. If we may judge the thought of the
Hellenists from the words of Stephen, one of their leaders (Acts
6:5), the Hellenists represented a vibrant theological movement
in early Christianity, with roots both in Jewish sectarianism and
in the diaspora. This movement was opposed to the domination
of Judaism by Jerusalem and saw in Christianity the signs of a
divine rejection of the Jerusalem Temple and some of its practices.[36] Probably the friction about the distribution of goods
that rose between the Hebrew Christians and the Hellenist
Christians (6:1) reflected a deeper quarrel between Christians
loyal to the Temple (see p. 17 above) and the radical Hellenists.
The decision to give the Hellenists their own leaders (men who
unfortunately have been misunderstood to be deacons) represented a choice in early Christianity for a pluralism on the question of relations to the Temple, rather than a policy of imposing
conformity. The implications of this decision were quickly felt
when a persecution broke out: the Hellenist Christians were
scattered while the apostles (presumably Hebrew Christians and
loyal to the Jerusalem Temple) were not bothered (8:1). Thus,
the Hellenists became the earliest missionaries, bringing Christianity with them as they moved. It was no accident that Philip,

---

[36] See O. Cullmann, *Expository Times* 71 (1959-60), pp. 8-12,
39-43—an English translation of his article "L'opposition contre le
Temple de Jérusalem."

a Hellenist, had great success in Samaria (8:5-6) where the inhabitants adhered to the Law of Moses but hated Jerusalem (see John 4:20).

The second major decision is narrated in Acts 15:1-12,[37] namely, the decision to accept the Gentiles without imposing on them the Law of Moses, especially circumcision. Acts shows a gradual opening of the Christian community to those who were outside Judaism, strictly defined. Philip converted Samaritans. Peter converted a Gentile who was favorable to Judaism (10:2). But Paul and Barnabas created a new problem by the fact that they converted large numbers of Gentiles who had no previous attraction to Judaism. At least some of the implications of such mass conversions must quickly have become obvious, especially as to weakening the bonds that bound the Christian movement to Judaism.[38] Thus, the decision reached in Jerusalem in 49 in reference to the legitimacy of these conversions was a decision not only as to how widely the Christian faith would spread but also as to the very nature of Christianity.

Acts shows the Twelve apostles as having an important role in each of these crucial decisions. The structure for making the decisions is noteworthy. In 6:2 the Twelve call together "the multitude" *(plēthos)* of the Jerusalem Christians; the apostles propose a solution to the problem of the Hellenists; this solution pleases the multitude who then choose the Hellenist leaders

------

[37] I follow the common critical view that Acts 15:1-29 has combined the accounts of two meetings at Jerusalem: (a) one at which Peter and the other members of the Twelve presided and where the decision confirmed Paul's stance that the Gentile converts were not bound by the law of circumcision—see Gal 2:1-10; (b) another in which James ruled that for Antioch, Syria, and Cilicia certain Jewish customs would be binding on Gentile Christians. Presumably this second meeting followed an argument at Antioch between Peter and Paul about such customs—see Gal 2:11-14. Paul's absence from the second meeting is implied by Acts 21:25 where he is informed of the rules made at the meeting.

[38] The ultimate (and unfortunate) implication, namely, that Christianity would become a separate Gentile religion, rejecting and rejected by Judaism, would not have been apparent so early—see p. 18 above.

and present them to the apostles. In Acts 15:4 the apostles and
presbyters welcome Paul and Barnabas to Jerusalem; but when
some of the Pharisee Christians challenge Paul's acceptance of
the Gentiles without circumcision, the multitude is called together with the apostles and the presbyters. Peter presents his
solution, and he is followed by Barnabas and Paul, while the
multitude listen in silence. The outcome (which favored Paul)
is described only confusedly because Luke has added here an
account of another meeting in Jerusalem in which James presided (see note 37 above). But almost certainly, as in Acts 6,
the multitude had to join with the Twelve[39] in giving approval
to the position defended by Peter and Paul. In Luke's description, then, the Twelve emerge as a type of council, presiding
over the multitude when meetings are called affecting the destiny
of Christianity. We have already stressed that the Twelve were
not local church leaders; now it becomes clear that for Luke
their concern was rather with the Church at large.

How plausible is this Lucan picture of the Twelve? Some
have assumed that Luke invented it in order to show that those
who were with Jesus during his ministry determined the policies
of the Church afterwards, and in this manner Luke created a
living chain binding the later Church to Jesus. Luke may well
have had this interest (although such an understanding really
comes more from reading between the lines than from what
Luke actually says); nevertheless, after the discovery of the
Dead Sea Scrolls we have to be more wary in speaking of Lucan
invention regarding the Jerusalem community. The group of
Jewish sectarians at Qumran responsible for the scrolls had a
form of community government remarkably like what Luke
describes in Acts 6 and 15. At Qumran the Assembly of all the
mature members of the community, called "the Session of the
Many" *(rabbîm),* was called together to exercise judicial and
executive authority over the sectarians. In addition, there was a
permanent community Council, consisting of twelve men and

---

[39] In Gal 2:9 Paul reports that "the pillars" of the Jerusalem
community, James, Cephas (Peter) and John (son of Zebedee),
gave him the right hand of fellowship. Two of the three pillars are
members of the Twelve.

three priests, which served as a higher and authoritative body within the general Assembly.[40] The parallel between "the many" of Qumran and "the multitude" of the Jerusalem Christians is obvious, as is the similarity of the council of twelve men in each group (probably patterned on the same idealism of the twelve tribes of Israel and the twelve patriarchal progenitors—with Qumran having additional representatives of the three clans of Levi). Thus, the Christian sect of Jews in Jerusalem may well have structured its government in imitation of other Jewish sectarians. If this comparison has any truth, then there is plausibility in the basic Lucan picture that in the primitive Church the Twelve constituted a type of council, convoking sessions to deal with major problems. After delineating another view of apostleship, we shall return to discuss whether and how the subsequent Church preserved this function ascribed by Luke to the Twelve.

B. Bishops and the Pauline Picture of Missionary Apostles

That Paul's view of the apostle was different from the Lucan view is undeniable. For Luke, the Twelve were the apostles *par excellence* because they were Jesus' chosen companions during his ministry. Even though Paul could not meet such a criterion, he argued vehemently that he was an apostle. In fact, it is from outbursts defending his apostolate against opponents (perhaps precisely on the point that he was not an original follower of Jesus) that we can put together some of Paul's ideas about apostleship. There can be detected at least three essential elements in Paul's concept of his apostleship: (a) he saw the risen Christ and was called by him; (b) he was sent on a mission to the Gentiles; (c) in his own life he imitated the death and resurrection of the Lord.

---

[40] F. M. Cross, Jr., *The Ancient Library of Qumran* (revised Anchor edition; Garden City, N. Y.: Doubleday, 1961), p. 231.

1. *The Pauline and Lucan Apostles Compared*

Some scholars have maintained that Paul's understanding of an apostle would have led him to deny the apostleship of the Twelve—a counterpart to the disputed thesis discussed above (p. 49) whereby Luke's idea of an apostle would have led him to deny Paul's apostleship. Once again, the dialectic is too sharp. Paul certainly admitted the apostleship of Cephas (Peter), as we see from Gal 1:18-19; 2:7. It is true, of course, that among the Twelve Peter was closest to being a missionary and, therefore, closer than the others to the Pauline ideals. But it is not certain that Paul had so narrow an understanding of missionary activity that he would not have considered that a mission had been entrusted to the Twelve, even though they remained in Jerusalem. As we saw (p. 27 above), all the Gospels include a missionary charge of the risen Jesus addressed to the Twelve; and since the charge varies in wording, the basic idea of a charge antedated any of the formulas now used to express it. In other words, the idea that the Twelve were sent by the risen Jesus must have been ancient, and there is no evidence that Paul would have wanted or been able to challenge it. Indeed, the fact that Paul mentions an appearance of the risen Jesus to the Twelve in a passage (I Cor 15:5-10) where he is trying to prove his own apostleship *may* be a tacit indication that he accepted the Twelve as apostles. In Gal 1:17 Paul makes reference to those in Jerusalem "who were apostles before me" (i.e., before his conversion). To whom would this refer if it did not at least include the Twelve?

I would go even further and suggest that Paul would have admitted, grudgingly perhaps, to a certain eminence of the Twelve among the apostles. That admission is implied in a backhanded manner in Paul's claim that, even though he was the least of the apostles, he was still an apostle (I Cor 15:9), and in the annoyed reference in Gal 2:9 to James, Peter, and John (two of them members of the Twelve) "who were reputed to be pillars."[41] The fact that Paul had to go up to Jerusalem

---

[41] James was not one of the Twelve, but he was probably an apostle by Pauline standards (Gal 1:19; I Cor 15:7).

over the question of admitting Gentiles, lest somehow he had run in vain (Gal 2:2); the fact that he held up as a model to his Gentiles the churches of God that were in Judea (I Thess 2:14); and the fact he spent so much time raising a collection of money for Jerusalem (p. 29 above), partly as his own peace offering —all this would imply that Paul's ideas were not totally contradictory to Luke's and that there was authority and power in Jerusalem because the Twelve were there.

Nevertheless, there can be no doubt that Paul's emphasis in speaking of apostleship differed so significantly from Luke's that we may speak of two concepts of apostleship with very diverse implications. The Lucan apostle, since he was a companion of Jesus, had his strength as a guarantor to the tradition handed down from Jesus. While this role is never spelled out in Acts, it is implicit in subsequent Church evaluation of the Twelve as men who spoke with authority because they knew the mind of the earthly Jesus. But Paul's knowledge of the earthly Jesus was second-hand, and that may be why he so seldom resorted to the words of Jesus (rare examples: I Cor 7:10-11; 11:23-26) —it would have been the area where he was weak and could make a mistake and thus be vulnerable to criticism by those who were apostles before him. Rather he had to solve problems on the implications of his vision of the risen Jesus, i.e., on the implications of the Christ-event. For instance, I think it no coincidence that it was Paul who brought the Gentile problem to the fore. It is true that Acts shows Peter converting Cornelius, a Gentile favorable to Judaism; but clearly Peter was surprised by what happened and could justify it only on the principle of the uncontrollability of the Spirit. The admission of Gentiles without strict adherence to the Mosaic Law was not a problem that one could solve by appealing to the words of the earthly Jesus; for while Jesus may have said that men would come from East and West to the heavenly banquet, his words need convey little more than the prophetic dream of the salvific subjection of all peoples to Yahweh (and the renewed Israel). Jesus' sayings during the ministry give no explanation of how to bring the Gentiles into God's kingdom, nor do they clearly take into account a Church or a long-lived Christian community. One may suppose that those "Pharisee" Christians who opposed the admission of Gentiles without circumcision argued precisely from the example of the earthly Jesus who himself worked within the framework of Judaism. There are Gospel sayings that confine Jesus' activity to the lost sheep of the house of Israel (Matt 15:24) and instruct his disciples to do likewise (10:5-6). When Paul argued for the admission of Gentiles without circumcision, as far as we know, he did not take up the question of the mind of the Jesus of the ministry; rather he based himself on the implications of God's action in the death and resurrection of Jesus —since Jesus was put to death as a violator of the Law, his death avails those who are outside the Law, etc. If we may generalize from the example of Paul, the missionary apostle would have tended toward theological innovation. Although he would have had a deep respect for the tradition (I Cor 7:10), his missionary activity would have brought him face to face with problems not encountered or foreseen in established Christianity; and such problems would have had to be solved on the basis of the implications of Christianity. However, lest we emerge with too polarized an image of the tendencies of the Pauline and Lucan apostles, it is worth noting that according to both Galatians and Acts the authorities in Jerusalem sided with Paul. And so the Twelve, the guarantors of the tradition, did not interpret the tradition in so narrow a fashion as did the Pharisee Christians who were Paul's opponents. An intelligent interpretation of tradition should enable one to recognize legitimate innovation.

Another feature in which the Pauline apostle differed from the Lucan concerns the care of individual churches. Like the Twelve Paul was not a local bishop; but as a missionary he founded churches for which he continued to be pastorally concerned, even though, in some instances, those churches had their own leaders. If according to Luke the Twelve were attentive to matters and decisions that affected the course of the whole Church, Paul was attentive to the behavior of his children in the churches he had evangelized. (It is noteworthy that in Rom 15:20 Paul is careful to state that he does not build on another man's foundations: he has to justify his letter to the Romans, for theirs was not a church he had founded.)

2. The Apostle Paul and Bishops

We have seen the historical difficulties raised by the claim that the NT presbyter-bishops were successors of the Twelve apostles. How does that claim fare in reference to the Pauline apostle? In many ways the presbyter-bishop differs from the Pauline apostle, so that we may not speak of succession in terms of identical functions. For instance, on two of the essential elements in Paul's understanding of an apostle (p. 59 above), the presbyter-bishop would be deficient: he had not seen the risen Jesus and was not commissioned by him. Also, as I pointed out in Chapter One, the character traits and mental outlook required of a residential episcopate are different from and sometimes opposed to those likely to be found in a missionary apostleship. As for possible sacramental succession, we remain in ignorance, since the NT is virtually silent on Paul's presiding at the Eucharist and totally silent on the presbyter-bishop's presiding. Thus, we are in the realm of surmise if we assert that Paul communicated sacramental power to bishops by ordination.[42]

---

[42] Some have found proof for the apostolic ordination of bishops in the Pastoral Epistles (a proof that would be seriously qualified if the Pastorals are not by Paul and represent an idealized retrojection from a later Church situation). In II Tim 1:6 Paul writes to Timothy: "I remind you to rekindle the gift of God that is within you through the laying on of my hands." However, since there is no evidence that Timothy was a bishop, the reference here is probably to ordination as apostolic disciple or apostolic delegate. If we add I Tim 4:14: "Do not neglect the gift you have, which was given you by prophetic words when the presbyters laid their hands upon you," we get a picture of Paul and other men of seniority, acting as Christian prophets, in selecting Timothy for a missionary task—in short, a scene similar to that of Acts 13:1-3 where the prophets and teachers of Antioch select two of their number, Barnabas and Saul (Paul), lay hands on them, and send them off to accomplish the mission for which the Holy Spirit has called them. A better text for

However, once these important differences have been noted, there is justification for the claim that the presbyter-bishops succeeded to the Pauline apostle in terms of pastoral care. As we see from Acts, the Pastoral Epistles, and the letters of Ignatius of Antioch, in some of the churches that Paul and his companions founded, there soon emerged presbyter-bishops who continued the care for the flock that had initially been exercised by the apostle. How did this come about? Did the apostle himself appoint presbyter-bishops when he was leaving a community (a procedure that would give basis for the idea of ordination)? Or are we talking about two roles separated by a generation—when apostles died off, did there emerge local leaders who filled in the power or authority gap? Or was it a case of both processes? These questions cannot be answered with certainty, but let us survey the evidence.

If we could depend with complete confidence upon the Book of Acts, our questions would be easily answered. As early as Paul's "First Missionary Journey" (*ca.* 48) Luke has Paul and Barnabas appointing presbyters in the newly evangelized churches (Acts 14:23). Near the end of Paul's "Third Missionary Journey" (*ca.* 58), during which he had spent about three years at Ephesus, Paul is pictured as having sent for the presbyters of Ephesus (Acts 20:17) whom he tells to feed the flock "over whom the Holy Spirit has set you as bishops" (20:28).[43] Thus, in Luke's view, it was Paul's ordinary pro-

---

the apostolic ordination of *bishops* would be I Tim 5:22 where Paul instructs Timothy not to be hasty in laying hands on men lest he thus participate in their shortcomings. If we may judge from Titus 1:5-7, with its instruction to appoint presbyters who seemingly are bishops, presbyter-bishops may have been among those men upon whom Timothy was to lay hands. While I have spoken of "ordination" in reference to the laying on of hands, it should be mentioned that this ceremonial action in the NT has implications far wider than installation into a church office; it is used for the transmission of divine power, as in healing, and for the communication of the Holy Spirit and special charisms.

[43] If Luke is accurate, we still have to allow the probability that the presbyter-bishops of the 40's and 50's did not yet have the official position or all the functions of the presbyter-bishops of the

cedure to leave behind presbyter-bishops in the communities where he worked. However, many scholars think that Luke has retrojected into the 40's and 50's the Church structure that existed later (80's?) when Acts was being written. They point out that in his own letters Paul never mentions presbyters in his churches—although all must acknowledge that Philip 1:1 mentions the existence of bishops in a church Paul had founded (perhaps only six years previously, if Philippians was written from Ephesus *ca.* 56) and thus raises the possibility that Paul had appointed these bishops. In order to evaluate the information supplied by Acts and to know whether it is confirmed by Philip 1:1 we must seek the answers to two questions: In Paul's time was there a distinction between presbyters and bishops? Does Philippi exemplify normal Pauline church structure?

The first question concerns the distinction between presbyters and bishops. It is generally admitted that in Acts, I Peter, and the Pastoral Epistles the titles are at least partially interchangeable. We have just seen that in Acts 20:28 Paul addresses the presbyters of Ephesus as "bishops." I Peter 5:1 is directed to presbyters who in 5:2 are said "to be exercising supervision" *(episkopein)*.[44] The Pastorals (see discussion of authorship below) speak of "the bishop" in the singular (I Tim 3:1-7; Titus 1:7-11) and of "presbyters" in the plural (I Tim 5:17-19; Titus 1:5). But since most commentators understand the singular usage to be generic, there is general agreement that we do not have here an instance of communities with only one bishop. The juxtaposition of Titus 1:5 ("Appoint presbyters in every

---

Pastorals (80's?). This caution about possible development should be kept in mind in reading my remarks above which are more directly concerned with the *origins* of the presbyter-bishops.

[44] While this is the best reading, the verb is missing in some important witnesses. The textual problem is not crucial since the general description of the presbyters in I Peter 5:1-4 fits presbyter-bishops quite well (especially the use of shepherd symbolism as in Acts 20:28-29). It is to be noted that the dating of I Peter (and implicitly authorship by Peter) is disputed, with the 60's and 80's being the most likely possibilities.

town") and 1:7 ("For a bishop must be . . .") would suggest
that "bishop" is simply a title for the presbyters in their pastoral
role. The possibility that only some presbyters functioned as
bishops is raised by I Tim 5:17: "Let the presbyters who rule
well be considered worthy of double honor."

If, then, in these instances we are justified in speaking of
presbyter-bishops, how is the double title to be explained? Some
scholars would see behind it a late 1st-century amalgamation of
once separate ecclesiastical roles. It is suggested that presbyters
existed in the Jewish Christian churches, in imitation of the
presbyters or elders of the synagogues, while the Gentile
churches, influenced by Greek customs (see note 22 above),
had bishops (*episkopoi,* "overseers"). This theory is question-
able on several grounds.

(a) The NT gives so little information on the subject that
affirmations about differences between Jewish and Gentile
Christian church structures are little more than guesses. While
presbyters are not mentioned in the certainly genuine Pauline
Epistles (i.e., Pastorals left aside), we are far from certain that
there were no presbyters in Paul's churches. The earliest Pauline
letter, written in 51, speaks of "those who *labor* among you and
rule over you in the Lord and admonish you" (I Thess 5:12).
Were these men presbyters? The verbs that we have italicized
are used of presbyters in I Tim 5:17. Were the "bishops" of
Philip 1:1 presbyter-bishops? As we saw, it is only rather inci-
dentally that Luke has Paul address the presbyters of Ephesus
as bishops (Acts 20:28—the only mention of bishops in Acts).
Without that coincidence many scholars would undoubtedly
theorize that Luke knew nothing of bishops and that the presbyters mentioned in the Gentile churches of Acts were distinct
from the (later) presbyter-bishops. The contention that the
bishops mentioned by Paul in Philippians (sole occurrence)
were not presbyters is a similar and dangerous use of the argument from silence. On the other side of the picture, the fact
that bishops are not mentioned in reference to the Jewish
Christian churches is not persuasive proof that those churches
had no bishops. Our chief proof that they had presbyters comes
from Acts which frequently mentions the presbyters of Jeru-

salem.[45] Was Jerusalem typical of the Jewish Christian churches, or was its structure complicated by the presence of James? Can we be sure from Acts that the presbyters of Jerusalem were not presbyter-bishops, when we find out coincidentally in the same book that the presbyters of Ephesus were?

(b) The theory that, unlike the presbyters who had Jewish antecedents, the bishops had Greek functionaries as antecedents has been called into question by a recent discovery. It is quite true, of course, that we cannot trace the bishops to the presbyters or elders of the Jewish synagogues, i.e., the council of senior men of stature who were looked to for counsel and who guided the direction of the community. As described in the NT, bishops exercised a more directly authoritative role; indeed the word *episkopos,* from *episkopein,* "to look over," means "overseer, supervisor, superintendent." As we saw in Chapter One, this superintendency included doctrinal and moral supervision and a managerial ability. If in our search for background we turn from the synagogues to the Jewish sectarian community at Qumran, of whose life we read in the Dead Sea Scrolls, we find a very close parallel to the Christian bishop—a parallel all the more impressive because we have already seen plausible Qumran sectarian influence on the structure of the Jerusalem church with its "multitude" and the Twelve. In the sectarian rule of life (1QS) the official who presided over the community Assembly was called "the Supervisor of the Many" (see p. 58 above)—the Hebrew terms used are *mᵉbaqqēr* and *pāqîd.*[46] An-

---

[45] Acts 11:30; 15:2, 6, 22, 23; 16:4; 21:18. James (5:14), almost certainly directed to a Jewish Christian community (where?), mentions the "presbyters of the church" who are to pray over the sick man and anoint him.

[46] Scholars are uncertain about the extent to which these terms are interchangeable. A passage in 1QS 6:12 speaks of "the Supervisor [*mᵉbaqqēr*] of the Many," while in 6:14 there is a reference to "the one who presides [verbal form related to *pāqîd*] at the head of the Many." Presumably these titles refer to the same person. However, in CD 14:6-9 a distinction is made between "the Supervisor [*mᵉbaqqēr*] over all the camps" and "the priest who is made to preside [verbal form related to *pāqîd*] at the head of the Many." Cf. F. M. Cross (work cited in note 40), p. 233, n. 81.

other Qumran document (CD or the Damascus Document) seems to describe a somewhat different form or stage of sectarian life in which there are smaller communities or camps; this document provides for a supervisor in each camp as well as one over all the camps. There are several striking points of similarity to the Christian bishop. *First*, there is a terminological parallelism. In the Greek OT, words related to *episkopein* are used to translate words from the Hebrew roots *bqr* and *pqd* which are at the base of the Qumran titles *mᵉbaqqēr* and *pāqîd*. Indeed, *pāqîd* is the perfect Hebrew equivalent of *episkopos*. *Second*, there is a parallelism of function. The Qumran *mᵉbaqqēr* is responsible for community property; Titus 1:7 refers to the bishop as an *oikonomos* ("steward") and I Tim 3:4-5 stresses that the bishop must be an efficient manager of his house. The Qumran supervisor selects and instructs candidates in the sectarian interpretation of the Law of Moses and judges the membership as to how they live up to the Law; Titus 1:9-10 speaks of the bishop's duty to hold firm to the doctrine he was taught so that he may give instruction and refute those who are insubordinate. The sermon to the presbyter-bishops of Ephesus in Acts 20:29-31 warns them to be on their guard against false teachers who will arise within the community.[47] *Third*, there is a parallelism of symbolism. We are told that the *mᵉbaqqēr* in each camp is to be like the shepherd of the flock tending the sheep in distress (CD 13:9-10); the same imagery of shepherding is used of the Christian presbyter-bishops in Acts 20:28 and I Peter 5:2-4.

On the basis of this evidence, it is possible to theorize that in Christian communities the custom of having presbyters or elders, which derived from the Synagogue, was reshaped and

---

[47] In light of the later development of the presbyter-bishop into the Christian priest, a few other details about the Qumran supervisor may be mentioned. Our evidence points to his being a priest or a levite. When Josephus (*War* II, 123) writes in Greek about how the Essenes (presumably the Qumran sectarians) chose their supervisor (whom he calls *epimelētēs*, "manager"), he uses the verb *cheirotonein*—the same verb *Didache* 15:1 uses to describe the choice of bishops.

modified by the example of another institution taken over from sectarian Judaism, namely, the more direct role of the supervisor. The result would be presbyter-bishops, and such a development suggests an earlier rather than a late origin of these functionaries. Obviously this thesis of origin militates against the contention that, at first, bishops were to be found only in Gentile Christian churches.[48]

We entered this discussion of the regional distinction between presbyters and bishops that is supposed to have existed in Paul's lifetime in order to test the veracity of Luke's claim that Paul appointed presbyters (= presbyter-bishops), a claim that has implications for succession to the apostles. If the distinction were verified and there were no presbyters in the Pauline Gentile churches, but only bishops, Luke's evidence could be dismissed. However, from what we have seen above, it would seem objective to state that the evidence for the regional distinction is minimal and that the Qumran parallelism offers another explanation for the origins of the episcopate that makes the combined presbyter-bishop a *possibility* in Paul's lifetime. Thus, Luke's evidence is not so easily dismissed. Yet, even if Acts is right and Paul did appoint presbyter-bishops in his communities, we still have to ask whether this was his universal practice; and so we are led to our next question.

The second question is whether Philippi with its bishops exemplifies the structure of the typical Pauline church. We could give an affirmative answer if we were sure that Paul wrote the Pastoral Epistles (I-II Timothy and Titus), for these writings point to the presence of presbyter-bishops in Ephesus and Crete. The traditional view that Paul wrote these letters in the

---

[48] H. Küng, *The Church*, p. 400, dismisses the thesis of Qumran parallelism "on the grounds that these 'bishops' existed at first only in the Greek communities." Such "grounds" are far from certain and indeed represent almost circular reasoning. Yet, even were one to concede them, possible derivation of the episcopate from Jewish sectarian models is not ruled out. Some of the closest parallels in the NT to Qumran thought are found in writings associated with the Gentile churches in Asia Minor (Colossians, Ephesians, Johannine writings).

mid-60's would mean that from Paul's lifetime we have confirmation of the picture of the church structure offered by Acts.
However, the majority of critical scholars today (with an in-
creasing number of Catholics included) question Pauline authorship and think of the Pastorals as pseudonymous. A moderate
compromise theory would be that the epistles were written by
disciples of Paul in the 80's or 90's to show what Paul's mind
would have been at this later period. According to such a theory
the Pastorals would agree with Acts because both writings
represent the post-Pauline church situation in the last decades
of the century. While we cannot be certain, it is probably best
to work with this latter theory.

If we set aside the Pastorals as witnesses for Paul's lifetime,
then we have little evidence with which to answer the question
we are asking about Philippi. However, a serious objection to
the thesis that all Pauline churches had bishops is offered by the
situation at Corinth. Paul's correspondence with Corinth is more
abundant than his correspondence with any other church; yet
he never mentions the presence of bishops at Corinth. In this
instance the argument from silence has more force than usual.
For example, if Corinth had bishops, could Paul have omitted
them from his long list of divine appointments in the church (I
Cor 12:28—unless bishops are to be identified with those listed
as having the charism of administration)? Could he have failed
to appeal to the authority of the bishops in the many instances
of church disorder that he had to correct in the Corinthian
correspondence? (Unless, of course, the bishops were the ones
who were responsible for the bad practices—an alternative that
those who argue for the presence of bishops at Corinth are not
usually willing to accept.) Thus, I think a plausible case can be
argued for the existence of a Pauline church that had no
bishops.

However, even if this is true, can one generalize from the
Corinthian situation to the majority of the Pauline churches of
the 50's? Scholars often contend that Corinth (no bishops) was
the rule and Philippi (bishops) was the exception. I wonder if
the likelihood is not in the other direction. In the history of the
first two Pauline missionary journeys Corinth was somewhat

exceptional in that it was the one church where Paul was able to spend a long time (a year and a half). It would seem quite likely that in places where Paul had been able to spend only a few weeks or a month (as at Philippi and perhaps Thessalonica[49]), upon departure he would have had to appoint leaders in order to insure the survival of what he had begun. But perhaps Paul felt that Corinth could survive without such structure because there he had been able for a longer time to nurture what he had planted and he knew how abundant were the gifts of the Spirit within that community. In any case, five years after the founding of the Corinthian church we find Paul in his correspondence having to act almost as if *he* were its bishop.[50] He has to write several critical letters about community life (more letters than have been preserved); he has to make one or more short visits, coming over from Ephesus to bring things back to order; he has to send emissaries to be sure his commands are obeyed. If Corinth was an experiment in leaving a church without formal local leadership, the experiment failed. (Indeed, we know that presbyter-bishops were eventually introduced into Corinth, for they are in existence when Clement of Rome writes to the Corinthians at the end of the century. Since Clement gives the Corinthian presbyter-bishops support, especially as to their place in worship and their not being easily removed from office, one may surmise that the introduction of such officials into Corinth was not without friction. He mentions in 42:4 that the apostles appointed bishops in the cities where they preached— might that suggest that after the Corinthian correspondence in 56-57 Paul introduced bishops into Corinth when he visited

---

[49] Paul may have spent somewhat more time at Thessalonica than is indicated in Acts 17:2. No bishops are mentioned in the Thessalonian correspondence, but Paul does refer to "those who labor among you and rule over you in the Lord and admonish you" (I Thess 5:12)—a terminology that, as we have mentioned, is used of presbyters (presbyter-bishops) in I Tim 5:17.

[50] More than elsewhere in the Pauline correspondence, the Corinthian letters are concerned with moral and sacramental problems in the church. One gets the impression of a more direct interference in internal ecclesiastical life.

there in 58?) If this hypothesis has any validity, we may doubt that Corinth was typical of Paul's procedure as regards church structure. And since Paul would scarcely have wanted to repeat his experience with Corinth,[51] it is not impossible that the Corinthian experiment may have hastened the development of local leaders in the Pauline churches. Thus, the Lucan picture whereby Paul appointed presbyter-bishops during his lifetime, while simplified,[52] may be true in its essentials.

*   *   *

As a summary of our discussion of the NT evidence about apostles and bishops, these conclusions seem warranted. The presbyter-bishops described in the NT were not in any traceable way the successors of the Twelve apostles.[53] Although quite different in many ways from the Pauline missionary apostles, the presbyter-bishops did eventually succeed to these apostles in the exercise of pastoral care over the churches the apostles

---

[51] It is curious how many scholars discuss Corinth as if it were a model Pauline church. The reason why it is the subject of so much study is that Paul wrote more about it than about any other church, but precisely because its behavior was not model. This does not mean, however, that the later, highly institutionalized Church has nothing to learn by way of corrective from the Corinthian charismatic structure.

[52] The picture is simplified even further by Clement of Rome who asserts that the apostles who received the Gospel and their commands from Jesus Christ went forth to preach and appointed their first converts to be bishops and deacons, with the condition that if these should die, other approved men should succeed to their ministry (42:1-4; 44:1-2). Clement has combined the Twelve with Paul. The contention that this must be historical because it was written in 96, relatively few years after the events, is naive in its evaluation of historical memory.

[53] The claims of various sees to descend from particular members of the Twelve are highly dubious. It is interesting that the most serious of these is the claim of the bishops of Rome to descend from Peter, the one member of the Twelve who was almost a missionary apostle in the Pauline sense—a confirmation of our contention that whatever succession there was from apostleship to episcopate, it was primarily in reference to the Pauline type of apostleship, not that of the Twelve.

had founded. In some instances, at least, they were probably appointed by the missionary apostles, even though we have no proof that a church structure which included bishops was established by all missionary apostles or even that it was established in all the churches founded by any single missionary apostle (e.g., the seeming absence of bishops in Corinth and their presence in Philippi at the same period). It is quite plausible that when churches without presbyter-bishops ultimately established them, they did so in imitation of churches that already had them, but many times without any special apostolic appointment. And so the affirmation that all the bishops of the early Christian Church could trace their appointments or ordinations to the apostles is simply without proof—it is impossible to trace with assurance any of the presbyter-bishops to the Twelve and it is possible to trace only some of them to apostles like Paul. The affirmation that the episcopate was divinely established or established by Christ himself can be defended in the nuanced sense that the episcopate gradually emerged in a Church that stemmed from Christ and that this emergence was (in the eyes of faith) guided by the Holy Spirit. Personally, I do not think that tracing the appearance of the episcopate more directly to the Holy Spirit than to the historical Jesus takes away any dignity from bishops; and I suggest that, upon reflection, these conclusions will be scandalous chiefly to those who have never understood the real import of our oft-repeated boast that Christianity is a historical religion.

II. Succession in the Church to Apostolic Functions

Granted all the limitations that we have put on the thesis that in NT times the bishops were the successors of the apostles, the historical fact remains that both the Twelve apostles and the missionary apostles eventually disappeared from the ecclesiastical scene[54] and many of their functions were taken over by

---

[54] The term "apostle" continues to be used in the Church for some years after the first generation of apostles had died, in refer-

the bishops who remained. As we pointed out in Chapter One, bishops constituted an institutionalized office in a settled community, and even our own anti-institutional age has to admit grudgingly that institutions do last. The NT does not give too much evidence about the transition from a Church where the apostles ranked first to a Church where the bishops ranked first, but if we read between the lines of III John we have an interesting indication that the transition was not always smooth.

As long as apostles like Paul were alive, bishops in the churches founded by the apostles could exercise only limited control, for the apostle could always intervene with the authority of the founding-father e.g., the letter to the Philippians. Even after the death of the missionary apostles, their closest disciples (the "second-grade" apostles) would often be acknowledged as having some right to exercise pastoral supervision of local churches, since presumably they knew what the mind of the apostle would have been. If the Pastoral Epistles were not written by Paul, they illustrate how Timothy and Titus, who had been companions of Paul, could instruct presbyter-bishops and set up conditions for candidates to the episcopate. (Is the purpose of these epistles to establish the right of "second-grade" apostles to do this?) But somewhere in the course of the late 1st century the apostolic bloodline inevitably grew thin, and the intervention of the disciples of the apostles or the disciples of the disciples began to be rejected as interference. This seems to be the case in III John. The letter is written by "the presbyter"; there are many theories about what this title may have meant, but plausibly it refers to a distinguished disciple of an apostle.[55]

---

ence both to the disciples or helpers of the original apostles and to wandering evangelists (*Didache* 11:3-6). However, like most charismatic functions, this continued apostolate was open to abuses, so that *Didache* 11:6 has to warn against apostles who are false prophets. Finally, even these "second-grade" apostles disappeared, and henceforth the term was used only occasionally and symbolically for great missionaries.

[55] If the author of III John also wrote I John, the opening verses of the latter seem to imply an eyewitness tradition passed down in the community. In my commentary on John (cited in note 12

As we see from II John, this presbyter speaks with authority to more than one church; and seemingly he has emissaries who move from church to church, evangelizing but also reporting back to their master on the state of things in the churches (III John 5-8, 10, 12). However, in the instance of III John, the presbyter cannot write directly to the church, as he does in II John; for Diotrephes, who *ranks first* in the community addressed,[56] does not acknowledge the authority of the presbyter. In fact, he has ignored the presbyter's early letter(s) and will not allow the presbyter's emissaries into the church (vss. 9-10). Apparently we have here a local church leader asserting his independence, and all that the presbyter can do is to threaten to come and charge Diotrephes before the community with insubordination. There is no hint that the presbyter can dismiss the local leader. The absolute authority of the apostles over church leaders is gone.

The fact that by a process of elimination the bishops took over the essential functions exercised in the NT period by various types of apostles has been, as in the case of the priesthood which also combined once diverse roles, both a blessing and a weakness. Below I shall illustrate the resultant complexities in a *few* aspects of the episcopal task.[57]

A. Functional Succession to the Pauline Apostolate

We mentioned in Chapter One that the virtues expected of a presbyter-bishop were quite different from those found in an apostle like Paul. The presbyter-bishop, as a staid and settled man, would often not make a good missionary apostle; and a

---

above), I favored the thesis that the Johannine writers may have been disciples clustered around John, son of Zebedee.

[56] Do we have here the emergence of a single leader from among the presbyter-bishops, and thus the birth pangs of the "monarchical episcopate"?

[57] I think it wise deliberately to limit my applications here, not only because I am going beyond the biblical era, but because of my very restricted competency to deal with the intricacies of the contemporary episcopacy and of the global structure of the Church.

man like Paul would not necessarily make a good residential church leader. But by replacing the missionary apostles, the bishops have been expected to take on tasks that really run against the likely inclinations of men holding such a residential office. Let us examine the conflict in one area. We have said that the Pauline apostle had to face new problems raised by his mission and so in a way became the theological innovator. In the later Church it was the bishops who, by office, had to face new ecclesiastical and theological challenges, and so from the 2nd to the 5th centuries many of the great theologians of the Church were bishops.[58] Nevertheless, psychologically the pastoral care of an established community would tend to make a man more the preserver of sound doctrine (Titus 1:9) than the theological innovator; and after the 5th century the bishop-theologian has become a less and less frequent phenomenon (except in the instance of famous theologians who were made bishops). Yet the idea is firmly maintained that the bishops are the official theologians of the Church because they are the successors of the apostles.

I am not suggesting that this attitude is unfortunate or should be totally changed. The bishops have pastoral care, and ultimately all theology is meant to lead men closer to God, so that the connection between the bishop-pastor and theology is not accidental. If the final theological decisions were left to professional theologians, who frequently do not have pastoral care, a very important dimension might be lost. However, sometimes the role of the bishop as official theologian has been misunderstood, as if the episcopal office somehow substituted for theological investigation and gave the occupant a divine insight. I can remember an incident which happened just before Vatican II that illustrates the difficulty. A bishop, now deceased, was welcoming several Scripture scholars who had been invited into the diocese to address the clergy. He remarked that he envied the modern seminarians because they had good professors in Scripture, whereas his own course had been hopeless and con-

---

[58] In the Western church, for instance, Augustine has often been considered Paul's successor as *the* theologian.

sequently he never felt confident about even the exegesis needed for preaching. At the end of these kind words, he cautioned the scholars that they should advise the audience that their conclusions about Scripture were only opinions, for the bishops were the only official theologians of the Church and only they could speak authoritatively about Scripture. Here was a man innocently claiming that he could speak authoritatively about a subject in which, as he had just admitted, he had not even elementary competence!

The unexamined claim of apostolic succession can cause confusion about the theological role of the episcopate in several ways. Excellent bishops have put themselves in a vulnerable and even ludicrous position by making dubious theological pronouncements, not because they were proud men, but because they felt that as part of their apostolic office they must supply the answers to the dogmatic and moral problems of the time. On the other hand, precisely because the bishops are considered the successors of the apostles in doctrinal matters, they are often criticized by "advanced" clergy and laity for not taking the initiative in bringing Christian thought to bear on the problems of contemporary civilization and for not providing theological leadership. What is really being demanded is that a residential bishop measure up to the standard of an apostle like Paul who was not a residential bishop! Perhaps the tension caused by impossible expectations on both sides has been lessened by the example of Vatican II where we saw how bishops could discharge their theological duties by cooperating with theologians. The bishops at the Council became more and more open to learning from their theological advisors, and this learning catalyzed their own pastoral insights and sparked them to real leadership—a development that surprised and humbled the theologians. But sometimes this cooperative attitude was smothered when the bishop returned to isolation of his diocese and the consuming demands of the local church.

Perhaps then it would be wise for Catholics to affirm explicitly, and not merely implicitly, that in the modern Church some of the principal activities of the Pauline apostolate, especially as regards offering leadership to face new religious problems, have been taken over functionally by men and women who are not bishops—by theologians, by enterprising priests and religious who by circumstances are thrust into new situations, and by perceptive laity with their manifold competencies. In the complexities of a modern diocese the main activities of most bishops do not and cannot take this direction. They can meet their responsibilities, however, by properly consulting with those who are involved in theology, in evangelization, in new apostolates, etc. The continuation of the functions of the Pauline apostle is the responsibility of the Church as a whole. A formal aspect of that responsibility has been entrusted to the bishop, but his succession to apostolic functions is qualified by the Church situation of our times. Only by drawing upon the larger resources of the Church can he make that succession realistic.

B. Functional Succession to the Apostolate of the Twelve

The idea of succession is even more complicated when we turn to the functional continuation of the task of the Twelve, who in the Lucan portrait were involved in major decisions facing the whole Church. If bishops are local church leaders, how can they take care of the larger Church? At least two basic types of solution have been found. *One solution* is to have the various local bishops come together in councils, either regional or ecumenical. Regionally this has been effective, particularly in the earlier period; and it is a hopeful sign that regional councils are being revived today in the modified form of frequent meetings of the national hierarchies. On the international scale, however, ecumenical councils have not been and cannot be frequent enough to supply consistent or continuous leadership to the whole Church. *The other solution* is to give one bishop more authority than others, so that his concern is for an area of many dioceses rather than exclusively for a local church. Archbishoprics are an example of regional authority given to a single bishop. In recent centuries in the West the function of the archbishop has been largely symbolic, but after Vatican II we are seeing a revival of provincial structure. A better instance of bishops with care for the larger Church may be found in the great patriarchates of the East, and it is no accident that in the first Christian millennium some of the most important decisions about the direction of Christianity came from the patriarchs of Alexandria and Constantinople. The supreme example of giving a single bishop responsibility for the larger Church is the papacy to which we now turn our attention. (Here we shall discuss the papacy only under the rubric of how bishops are functionally successors to the Twelve.)

It is interesting that in exercising pastoral care for the universal Church the bishop of Rome claims to be successor of Peter. Of course, Peter was a unique figure among the Twelve; yet he was not divorced from the Twelve. In Acts he is pictured as the spokesman and leader of the Twelve in reaching authoritative decisions. His position as the foundation rock of the Church (Matt 16:18) is not without a parallel to the position of the Twelve apostles as the foundations of the walls of the heavenly Jerusalem (Rev 21:14). The authority of binding and loosing given to Peter (Matt 16:19) was given also to the Twelve (18:18). It is quite appropriate, then, that in Roman Catholicism the most obvious functional succession to the role Luke assigns to the Twelve (i.e., making decisions concerning the Church at large) is in one who claims succession to a member of the Twelve.

We have seen that there is no real proof that in NT times Peter would have been looked on as the bishop of the Roman community; and so theoretically, I suppose, the succession to his role as leader of the Twelve need not have been attached to a bishopric. But again, with the disappearance of apostles, bishops were the only leaders in the Church to whom major functions could be entrusted. Thus, the succession fell to the bishop of Rome, the city where Peter had died;[59] and this con-

---

[59] I eschew any attempt here to trace the complicated history of the beginnings of the papacy. It is fascinating that while the institution of the Twelve was not continued in the Church after their death (p. 55 above), the primacy of Peter was seen to be of continued importance and thus persevered in the Church. Note the emphasis given to Peter in Matt 16:17-18; Luke 22:32; and John 21:15-17—works written after Peter's death.

nection has been maintained even in the period when the bishops of Rome did not put foot in the city (Avignon period). However, the difficulty of reconciling the apostolic function of the Twelve with the activity of a local bishop has remained apparent. For all practical purposes the Pope exercises his episcopal obligations toward the city of Rome through delegates. Even though modern Popes have made sincere efforts to show their concern for Rome, the one man cannot be a deeply involved local bishop and take care of the universal Church at the same time.

The fact that the most obvious succession to the function of the Twelve is centered in *one* bishop who acts as successor to Peter is a concentration bound to produce difficulties, such as those that we are now encountering within Catholicism. If Peter was the chief of the Twelve, in Acts 6 and 15 he is not shown making the crucial decisions in isolation (either from the Twelve or from "the multitude"). In recent centuries, as the Popes themselves have come to realize, the bishop of Rome has been too isolated in making similar crucial decisions. Of course, when it functions well, the Curia is a means of broadening the papacy. This contribution will be greatly enhanced by Pope Paul's efforts at internationalizing the Curia. The Senate of Bishops is another very important step in broadening the functional succession to the Twelve. Still another step is Rome's effort to press residential bishops in Christian countries to assume responsibility for evangelization in missionary countries.[60]

Yet, in correcting the abuse of an isolated papacy, we should not be unappreciative of the strength given to the Church by that institution. The analogy between the role played by Jerusalem in Acts and the role played by Rome in the Church should not be wasted upon us. The functional succession to the Twelve has to be wider than the papacy and has to touch other bishops, but we shall always encounter the practical difficulty of effectively involving the heads of local churches in de-

---

[60] Previously Rome did not want individual dioceses to "adopt" missionary areas on the grounds that the missions were the responsibility of the universal Church (which meant a Roman curial congregation).

cisions that require a knowledge of the whole Church. The urge to decentralize and "debureaucratize" the Roman administrative processes should not obscure the fact that a church as large as the Roman Catholic Church cannot survive without considerable centralization. (And since I, for one, think that there cannot be a true Christianity without the Church, I do not think of the survival of the Church as merely the self-perpetuation of an institution.) Even more important, the laudable urge to make it possible for the papacy to become more representative of the theological and ecclesiastical complexities of various local churches should not lead us to consider the Pope merely as the spokesman for the consensus of the Church. The apostles in both the Lucan and the Pauline conceptions spoke to problems in the name of Jesus Christ, whether they did so in light of the tradition of Jesus' words or on the basis of the implications of the Christ-event. Answering problems in Jesus' name will run just as often against the consensus as in harmony with it. If the Church has to speak to the world, someone has to be able to speak for the Church. One of the greatest strengths of the Roman Catholic Church is that it clearly has someone who can speak for it. We should never cease striving that the Pope speak representatively for the Church, but what enormous damage would be done if we strive in such a way that we make his voice ineffective.

* * *

Many other aspects of functional succession to the apostles could be discussed, but the few instances mentioned exemplify well the conflicts caused by the fact that local bishops have been made heirs to the quite diverse activities of the Lucan and Pauline types of apostles. Perhaps as a result of a better historical understanding of why there are difficulties, Catholics shall be able to modify an often too simplistic concept of the bishops as the successors of the apostles and in so doing enable the bishops to serve more effectively and realistically as the formal representatives of an apostolic succession that must be shared more broadly.

III. The Ecumenical Implications

As mentioned in the Preface, these biblical reflections had as their catalyst not only problems within the Catholic Church but also the question of our ecumenical relations with other churches that do not possess an episcopate in historical succession to the apostles. On pp. 72–73 I have attempted to state the limits that the evidence imposes upon our understanding of the historical relationships between bishops and apostles in the NT period. The fact that the episcopate is seen as a structure that gradually developed in the Church rather than as something that was within the expressed directions of Jesus does not, in my opinion, reduce the episcopate to just another possible form of Church government. Episcopacy is intimately related to apostolicity which is an essential note of the Church. In its basic meaning apostolicity expresses the Church's fidelity to the apostles' proclamation of the Gospel and its continuation of their mission to bring men under God's rule (kingdom) as heralded by Jesus. An episcopacy that, at least in a limited way, is historically traceable to the apostolic period can function as a clear sign of apostolicity and as an effective means of preserving the continuity of apostolic proclamation and mission. Acts 20:28-30 and Titus 1:9-11 indicate that even in NT times one of the principal tasks of the episcopate was to preserve the apostolic teaching free from heresy. The lists of bishops that appeared in the late 2nd century (in particular, the lists of Roman bishops) were intended to demonstrate a line of legitimate teachers as a guarantee that the teaching of the churches represented faithfully the teaching of the apostles. The formalizing of ordination at the hands of the bishops served to make clearly recognizable those whom the Church had delegated to celebrate the Eucharist and thus to keep the sacramental tradition pure. Thus, the wisdom of the Holy Spirit in providing the Church with the episcopate has been manifested in many ways; and on a practical level, in moments of crisis it has been the solidarity of the episcopate with Rome that has preserved the unity of the Church. In the movement of Church reform officially initiated at Vatican II, naturally we think of a reform of the episcopate as well; but the whole goal of this reform is to increase the effectiveness of the episcopacy and not at all to encourage experiments that would substitute some other form of non-episcopal structure.[61]

Now, if we Catholics are deeply attached to the role of the episcopacy within our own Church as a preeminent sign of apostolicity and unity, what should be our attitude toward other Christian churches that have no episcopacy or, at least, no episcopacy in what we would consider historical succession? Are we forever to be separated from them unless they accept our episcopate? (Obviously I speak here of only one of the obstacles to Christian unity, and I am thinking of *the hypothetical situation where this obstacle remains after there has been real agreement on doctrine, sacraments, and other essentials of Christian life.*) The episcopate is a sign of apostolicity, but is it an essential of apostolicity? Or is fidelity to the apostles in basic doctrine and practice minimally sufficient for a church, without the visible connection to apostolic times inherent in episcopal succession? The episcopate is a powerful force for unity, but do we not find in some other churches different structures that also preserve unity? Many modern Catholic theologians are inclined to answer these questions in a way that would acknowledge the possibility of a non-episcopal church's possessing enough of the essential notes of apostolicity and unity to make church union or mutual recognition feasible.

It seems to me that our study of the NT picture points in the same direction. The likelihood that in Paul's lifetime some of his churches that had no bishops lived in fellowship with churches that had bishops suggests the possibility of two such churches living in union today. The probability that not all the presbyter-bishops of the years 80-110 could trace their position back to appointment or ordination by an apostle suggests the possibility of our openness to churches with an episcopate that (by our standards) is not in historical succession to the apostles.

---

[61] Undoubtedly "underground churches" think of themselves as reform movements; but when they totally separate themselves from the bishop, it is difficult to think of them in other terms than schismatic.

And since the process of appointment or ordination was almost certainly quite varied in the early centuries, it would seem that as regards sacred ministry a modern union need involve no more than the recognition by one church of those whom the other church designates as clergy, without demanding a reordination of the non-episcopally ordained clergy. Recognition by the church is what is essential for sacred ministry; ordination by the laying on of a bishop's hands is simply the standard way of conferring recognition in episcopally structured churches, and in the novel instance of church union an alternative form of recognition could be introduced, namely, a proclamation of the acceptance of validity by the Pope.[62] Correspondingly, the non-Catholic church would acknowledge Catholic priesthood and episcopate as a legitimate development from NT origins—an acknowledgment that would constitute an important corrective of Reformation polemics.

It may be objected that entry into union with a non-episcopal church without insisting on episcopal ordination is tantamount to admitting that one form of church government is as good as another. This is not necessarily true: such a union does not deny our belief that episcopacy evolved in the Church under the guidance of the Holy Spirit, but recognizes that through unfortunate historical circumstances some Christians have not been able to appreciate how the episcopacy serves as an effective

---

[62] Note the insistence on the role of the respective *churches*. On the part of the Roman Catholic Church, union with another community must involve careful investigation in order to be sure that our prospective partners would be one with us in the doctrinal and moral essentials of the Christian life. If this investigation proves satisfactory, then we should act as a church through our official spokesmen (the bishops and the Pope). The inclination of individual priests and laity to decide for themselves that the clergy of another church are validly ordained so that the Eucharist may be received from their sacramental tables may produce a feeling of being "really Christian" but, in fact, solves nothing and may jeopardize a permanent solution. If we are serious in contending that it is by Church consent that individuals are authentically designated to exercise a special ministry (pp. 41-42 above), then it is difficult to see how for Roman Catholics one could have such consent without ultimate action by the hierarchy.

sign of unity and apostolicity. In particular, we may think of the medieval period when bishops became lords or princes and when the absentee bishop was not exceptional. The lack of pastoral concern in this era turned many Christians against the bishops, and this reaction led some of the reformed churches to consider the episcopacy as a corruption of the Gospel rather than as an effective means of perpetuating it. We cannot expect such churches, which in the meantime have developed an alternative structure, suddenly to regain an appreciation of the episcopate, especially if our insistence on it prolongs the division of Christianity or if they are asked to accept a ceremony of episcopal ordination in which they have no real faith. Yet it is not inconceivable that in some instances, when union with an episcopal church has been realized, an interest in and an openness to the episcopate may develop on the part of the non-episcopal churches. Some Protestant churches are non-episcopal only because no bishops in historical succession to the apostles came with them at the time of their separation. Provided that episcopal structure is not demanded of them, such churches may ultimately adopt it—if it were demanded as of divine necessity, they would logically be forced to admit that their status for hundreds of years has been invalid.

Some profit may be gained in the other direction as well, if our Catholic Church would enter a union with less formally structured churches. There are dangers inherent in the episcopacy precisely because it is an institutionalized form of church government. Inevitably it will tend to become too rigid and too confining, to the point of frustrating the spontaneity of the Christian experience. The impression will be given that the Holy Spirit works only through the hierarchy, from the top down and never from the bottom up. As we read the NT, I think we are right in judging that the strongly charismatic community at Corinth was not a viably structured church. Yet we can learn from Corinth, not only negatively but also positively. If under the guidance of the Spirit, the Church, even in NT times, was led to a more viable, episcopal structure, it still cannot ignore the manifestation of the same Spirit in the charisms of Corinth. A respect for the charismatic element in Christianity, especially in terms of a willingness to see the movement of the Spirit out-side the hierarchical structure, is the best corrective for some of the innate perils of an episcopally structured church. This respect might be heightened for Catholics through church union.

In conclusion, then, I would join with the many Catholic spokesmen who believe deeply in the importance of the episco-pacy and yet do not think that a demand for its acceptance should be allowed to constitute an ecumenical obstacle—once again, in the hypothesis that other pertinent doctrinal differences have been resolved. The Church in NT times included both Corinth and Philippi, as well as the churches of the Pastorals—indeed it probably included many other unknown stages and forms of church structure. Even if the later Church was far less pluralistic as regards structure, the fact of Christian division since the Reformation has re-created a pluralism. Will the exigencies of our times permit us to be less ecumenical than the Church of the NT?